Jabberwock

Improbabilities lived and imagined by
James Thurber
In the fictional city of Columbus, Ohio

Made into a play by
Jerome Lawrence and Robert E. Lee

S A M U E L   F R E N C H, I N C.
45 West 25th Street   NEW YORK, N.Y. 10010
7623 Sunset Boulevard   HOLLYWOOD 90046
LONDON   *TORONTO*

In all programs and in all advertisements, authorship credit shall be given as follows: The title of the Play shall be immediately followed by the credit to the Author of the underlying material and the Authors of the Play in exactly the form in which it appears on the cover of the playbook. No person shall receive billing in larger type than that accorded to the Authors. Authorship credit shall also be given in connection with all publicity issued by the amateur producing group.

'Twas brillig, and the slithy toves
Did gyre and gimble in the wabe;
All mimsy were the borogoves,
   And the mome raths outgrabe.

"Beware the Jabberwock, my son!
The jaws that bite, the claws that
   catch!
Beware the Jubjub bird, and shun
   The frumious Bandersnatch!"

He took his vorpal sword in hand:
Long time the manxome foe he
   sought—
So rested he by the tumtum tree,
   And stood awhile in thought.

And as in uffish thought he stood,
The Jabberwock, with eyes of flame,
Game whiffling through the tulgey
   wood,
   And burbled as it came!

One, two! One, two! And through
   and through
The vorpal blade went snicker-snack!
He left it dead, and with its head
   He went galumphing back.

"And hast thou slain the Jabber-
   wock?
Come to my arms, my beamish boy!
O frabjous day! Callooh! Callay!"
   He chortled in his joy.

'Twas brillig, and the slithy toves
Did gyre and gimble in the wabe;
All mimsy were the borogoves,
   And the mome raths outgrabe.
                    —LEWIS CARROLL

* * * * *

What do you mean it **WAS** brillig?
                    —JAMES THURBER

The premiere performance of JABBERWOCK commemorated the opening of the THURBER THEATRE on the Ohio State University campus, Columbus, Ohio, November 18, 1972. The cast:

JAMIE THURBER .... *Robert Isenhart*
HERMAN THURBER .... *Michael Ayers*
CHARLIE THURBER .... *David Graf*
MARY AGNES THURBER .... *Rosemary Sauers*
ROY THURBER .... *Charles Shanks*
MR. BODWELL'S VOICE .... *Robert Swires*
MRS. BODWELL'S VOICE .... *Elizabeth Langford*
POLICE SERGEANT .... *David Grosshandler*
FIRST POLICEMAN .... *Howard Bowman*
SECOND POLICEMAN .... *William Corson*
THIRD POLICEMAN .... *Carl Welkom*
REPORTER .... *Roger Hall*
GRANDPA FISHER .... *David Ayers*
GET-READY MAN .... *Gregory Parker*
DOC MARLOWE .... *Alan Montgomery*
GEORGIANA LITTLEFIELD .... *Suzanne Shaner*
GENERAL LITTLEFIELD .... *T. Michael Hissam*
WAR BOND GIRL .... *Elizabeth Langford*
RECRUITING SERGEANT .... *Robert Zeeb*
R.O.T.C. CADETS .... *Jed Whitaker, Jerry Prell,*
                                    Michael Grimes
VOLUNTEERS .... *William Corson, Carl Welkom,*
                                         Fred Fate
ELECTRICIAN .... *Stanford Tipton*
PROFESSOR WELCH .... *Fred Fate*
DR. RIDGEWAY .... *Michael Schirtzinger*
DR. QUIMBY .... *Michael Grimes*
DRAFTEE .... *Jerry Prell*
MAILMAN .... *Fred Fate*
A SWARM OF AUNTS:
    AUNT ESTHER .... *Gwen Kagey*
    AUNT BELINDA .... *Jacqueline Stelzer*
    AUNT IDA .... *Ann Callis*

5

AUNT FANNY .... *Clara Ireland*
AUNT HANNAH .... *Brenda Fisher*
AUNT MINNIE .... *Cynthia Haynes*
AUNT CHARLOTTE .... *Florence Smith*
AUNT BESSIE .... *Bonita Jay*
AUNT SARAH .... *Victoria Rank*
A PRIDE OF MAIDS:
DORA GEDD .... *Marilyn Wise*
ELVIRA WEIR .... *Lynne Roth*
LILY LOOMIS .... *Dana Lovell*
GERTIE STRAUB .... *Jane Pepper*

Directed by *Roy Bowen*

Scene Design by *Russell T. Hastings*

Lighting Design by *W. Alan Kirk*

Costume Design by *Michelle Guillot*

The first professional production was at Dallas Theater Center as the pilot production of American Playwrights Theatre. Jerome Lawrence directed.

THE PLACE

The Thurber menage in Columbus, Ohio; also various haunts above, below and beyond High Street.

THE TIME

ACT ONE

When W. Wilson was keeping us out of war.

ACT TWO

When W. Wilson (Mary Agnes, Grandpa and others) were making the world safe for democracy.

6

THE CAST

Mary Agnes Thurber
Jamie
Herman
Roy
Charley Thurber
Grandpa Fisher
Doc Marlowe
Georgiana Littlefield
The Get-Ready Man
General Littlefield
Electrician
Professor Welch
Mr. Briscoe, *the Postman*
Dr. Ridgeway
Dr. Quimby
Draftee
Policemen, Carpenter, R.O.T.C. Cadets, Recruiting Sergeant, Reporter, Bond Sales-girl, Voices of the Bodwells

A Swarm of Aunts:
Aunt Esther
Aunt Belinda
Aunt Ida
Aunt Fanny
Aunt Minnie
Aunt Charlotte
Aunt Bessie
Aunt Sarah

A Pride of Maids:
Dora Gedd
Elvira Weir
Lily Loomis
Gertie Straub

7

(The AUNTS *and the* MAIDS *can be cast two different ways: ideally, they should be different actresses for each role. But the play is written so that one actress can make the changes and play all the aunts as a tour-de-force. The same is true of the maids.* LITTLEFIELD *and* WELCH *might double as the two* DOCTORS: *the* POLICEMEN *can double later as* ELECTRICIAN, RECRUITING SERGEANT *and* CADETS.)

Jabberwock

ACT ONE

AT RISE [*to coin a phrase*]: *Or, if you don't want to use a curtain, the authors have no objection. In which case, delete "At Rise." It is 2:00 A.M. Everybody in the Thurber house is asleep. Well, almost everybody. We see the house in X-Ray: the plumbing, the gas connections, the drain-pipes, gutters and downspouts. No walls.*

* * * *

Details of Set:

At stage level is the Living Room. R. is an Entry Hall, from which several steps angle down into the Living Room. The heavy oak front door, R., is adorned with Early-Ohio stained glass; outside is a stoop with steps descending to the street, directly front. A full-length oval picture frame, lit Sepia, like a daguerreotype, faces downstage in the Entry Hall. There is an umbrella stand and an undernourished fern in an urn. The front staircase leads upstairs and upstage from the Entry Hall, so anyone descending from the bedrooms above is plunging straight at the audience. Welsbach gas mantles in a chandelier crown the Living Room. An overstuffed couch is antimacassared. A two-piece telephone is nearby, with a long cord. Prominent by the main staircase and revered as a Family Bible is a well-thumbed Webster's Unabridged on a reading stand. A door L., leads from the Kitchen, to the back-stoop and backyard; it is a screen-door with an agonized coil spring, and it twangs and whams shut as only an Ohio screen-door can. A white enamel gas stove squats beside a 1902 ice-box which feeds on ice instead of making it. Whoever works at the Kitchen Sink and Counter is framed in a down-stage window; the flowerbox under it has one disenchanted geranium. There is a door leading upstage from the Kitchen to an unseen Maid's Room. All door frames should be solid, so the doors can be yanked open or slammed shut. A slightly chipped porcelain-topped kitchen table links the Living Room and the Cooking Area. There are several unpainted wooden chairs. A back-stairs climbs from the Kitchen to a landing. A door opens upstage of it to the unseen Bedroom of CHARLIE and MARY AGNES. Left of the landing is a door into the Bathroom, which has a sink, a bathtub with feet, and a gas light fixture. From this landing, a few steps leads up to the Attic, which is roughly Center and raked slightly. It contains a cozy old four-poster bed, quilted and goose-feathered. GRANDPA is asleep on the floor in a Civil War sleeping bag. A Corridor runs across the stage, from the top of the front stairs R., to the landing of the back-stairs, L. JAMIE and HERMAN sleep in two stoically small beds in the Bedroom, R.; JAMIE's bed is immediately above the oval picture frame. A door to ROY's unseen bedroom is upstage of the R. upper landing. The thrust area Downstage could be the Thurber's yard and the street outside. In the course of the play, it becomes the rest of Columbus, including several street-corners, Ohio State University, the Draft Board, and the banks of the mighty Olentangy River. Though the house is skeletonized, the Designer should resist the temptation to be "cartoon-y." There should be no painted flats, no scenic exaggerations or grotesqueries.

*   *   *   *

About the Play:

Though what happens in the play may strain credibility a bit, the people must be utterly credible. Messrs. Thurber, Lawrence and Lee are not even remotely related to M. Feydeau.

* * * *

AUNT ESTHER *is posed, primped for a photo, in the oval frame. She is frozen, motionless.* JAMIE *and* HERMAN *are in their beds.* GRANDPA *wheezes intermittently from the attic floor. After the applause for the set has died down,* JAMIE THURBER, *age 16-and-a-half, sits up in bed abruptly. His hair is a haystack from restless sleep. He squints around. Not having his glasses on, he doesn't see anything. As* JAMIE *gropes for his glasses, his hand bumps against* HERMAN, *age 13, in the adjoining bed.*

HERMAN. Awp.
JAMIE. Sorry, Herman. (HERMAN *doesn't wake up.* JAMIE *finds his glasses, puts them on. He makes a face as he runs his tongue over his teeth. He picks up a bath-towel from the floor, slings it around his middle as he gets out of bed. He opens the Bedroom door and shuffles along the dimly-lit corridor toward the Bathroom.* JAMIE *is no Bernarr McFadden. Along with the bath-towel he wears an eternal question-mark. He goes into the Bathroom, strikes a match and lights a gas-mantle over the sink. He stares into an imagined downstage mirror, sticks out his tongue at himself and bares his teeth to examine them.* CHARLEY THURBER [*Age 45*] *enters the front door into the shadowy Living Room.* JAMIE *has started to brush his teeth—but stops mid-stroke. Did he hear something below? He shrugs and continues brushing.* CHARLEY *is a tall, friendly man—but tonight he is just tired. He carries a small pasteboard suitcase. He crosses to the Kitchen.*

Without turning on any light, he goes to the ice-box and pulls out a half-full quart bottle of milk. While JAMIE *is brushing his teeth in the upstairs Bathroom, his* FATHER *is drinking a glass of milk in the downstairs Kitchen. As he puts the glass in the sink, his elbow brushes against the milk-bottle, which clatters noisily on the porcelain table top. The remaining inch of milk is spilled.* JAMIE *jumps at the sound, nearly biting his tooth-brush.* CHARLEY *mutters wearily, putting the milk-bottle in the sink. Apprehensive,* JAMIE *peers down the back stairs into the Kitchen. Simultaneously,* CHARLEY *stumbles over the suitcase, a chair clatters to the floor.* JAMIE *reacts sharply at the sound, races into his Bedroom and closes the door, holding it shut with his back. The boy has just missed seeing his Father, who with his suitcase, has climbed to the top of the back stairs. Seeing the gas-light burning in the Bathroom,* CHARLEY *reaches in, turns it off and plods sleepily through the door to his own Bedroom.*)

JAMIE. (*A scared whisper.*) Pssst! Herman—!

HERMAN. Awp.

JAMIE. Are you awake?

HERMAN. No.

JAMIE. Herman, something very peculiar is—

HERMAN. (*Sitting bolt upright.*) Who are you?

JAMIE. Jamie.

HERMAN. What are you doing in my room?

JAMIE. I sleep here.

HERMAN. Why aren't you sleeping?

JAMIE. My teeth woke me up. (HERMAN *is wearing flannel pajamas and is climbing laboriously to consciousness.*)

HERMAN. You're not wearing anything.

JAMIE. Sure I am. I'm wearing a towel.

HERMAN. Oh. (*He is starting to sink back to sleep.*)

JAMIE. (*Insistently.*) There's something downstairs.

HERMAN. Like what?

JAMIE. Like a noise. (*This rouses the younger* BOY.

JAMIE *pulls the reluctant* HERMAN *toward the head of the back stairs. They listen intently. Total silence.*)

HERMAN. *I* don't hear anything.

JAMIE. *I* did. A rattling. And a clanking. Then a thump. (*A pause.*)

HERMAN. Why doesn't one of us go down and see what it is?

JAMIE. Good idea. Go ahead.

HERMAN. You heard it. *You* go.

JAMIE. We'll go together. (*Scared, the two boys start slowly down the back staircase. Staring in opposite directions, they bump into each other, and a metal pan clatters to the Kitchen floor. Startled, the boys flee back up the stairs to their own Bedroom,* HERMAN *in the lead. The younger boy ducks into the Bedroom first, slams the door behind him, holding it shut with his knee.* JAMIE, *trapped outside, pounds on the door.*) Lemme in!

HERMAN. You're not gonna get me, you *thing!* You thing!

JAMIE. I'm not a "thing"! I'm your brother, for God's sake! (JAMIE *pounds some more, but* HERMAN *won't let him in.* MARY AGNES THURBER *emerges from her Bedroom,* L.)

MARY AGNES. What on earth are you boys up to?

JAMIE. (*Hoarsely.*) Nothing, Mama. (MARY AGNES THURBER *is a young and vigorous 43. If she had been on the bridge of the Titanic, it wouldn't have dared to go down. She seems always to be in motion, even when she's standing still.*)

MARY AGNES. What was all that running around downstairs?

JAMIE. You heard it, too—!

MARY AGNES. Burglars! (HERMAN *opens the door a crack to listen.*)

JAMIE. Shhh! They'll hear you!

MARY AGNES. I certainly hope so. (*Shouts.*) Get out of the house, you burglars!!! (MARY AGNES, *who knows no fear, starts down the back-stairs.*)

JAMIE. Careful, Mama—they might be armed!

MARY AGNES. (*Pulling off a slipper.*) So am I! (*Flinging a slipper down the stairs to the kitchen.*) Scat!

JAMIE. I don't think it's burglars.

MARY AGNES. What else *could* it be?

JAMIE. I'd rather not say.

MARY AGNES. Your Grandfather! (*She opens the attic door, hurries up the few steps, sees the empty bed.*) Omigod—! He's gone— (*Then she sees* GRANDPA *as he turns in his sleep on the Civil War sleeping bag. She comes back to* JAMIE.) It's all right. He's out on bivouac again. What are you doing in that towel?

JAMIE. If I didn't have this on, I'd be naked.

HERMAN. (*Trembling like Jell-o.*) I'm scared. Where's Papa?

JAMIE. In Indianapolis.

MARY AGNES. No-o-o. He got back *hours* ago. He was fast asleep when you woke me up.

JAMIE. (*Numbly, staring toward the bathroom.*) The gas-light's out in the bathroom.

MARY AGNES. Well, I should hope so.

JAMIE. But I just lit it. Something blew it out!

HERMAN. A ghost! (HERMAN *slams the door again, blocking it.*)

MARY AGNES. A ghost? Oh, I'd much rather it was a burglar. (ROY, *19, comes out of his Bedroom. He wears jazzy cotton pajamas and an old robe he outgrew three years ago.*)

ROY. (*Sleepily.*) What's going on?

MARY AGNES. I'm so glad you're up, Roy; you can go down and see what it is. (ROY *starts down, but immediately scampers up again.*)

ROY. What's "It"?

JAMIE. We don't know. Come on, Roy. I'll go down with you.

ROY. (*Chicken.*) I'll stay with Mama. She's all excited.

MARY AGNES. Don't any of you go anyplace. We'll call the police.

JAMIE. The phone's downstairs. (*They look at one another.*)

MARY AGNES. Well, there are other ways to communicate. (*She tries to enter the bedroom, still blocked by* HERMAN.) Herman, let me in!

HERMAN. Who is it?

ROY. (*Helping his Mother push the door open.*) Oh, for cripes' sake, Herman, stop being a baby. (*The boys follow as* MARY AGNES *strides into the room, takes off her other slipper and throws it through a window off* L. *It thuds against siding. She gropes under the bed for one of* JAMIE'S *shoes and hurls it with even more vigor.*)

JAMIE. Hey— (*There is a shattering of glass from off. A woman screams.*)

MR. BODWELL'S VOICE. (*Off.*) Burglars! Burglars! Burglars!

MARY AGNES. See? They've got burglars, too!

HERMAN. (*Green.*) Or ghosts!

MARY AGNES. (*Calling out the window.*) Mrs. Bodwell! Pick up your phone and call the police!

MRS. BODWELL'S VOICE. (*Off.*) Don't worry, Merle, we'll sell the house and move back to Peoria. (CHARLEY *comes out of the bedroom door, sleepily, in a night-shirt.*)

CHARLEY. Oh, it's good to get home to a nice peaceful house. (*Shouting.*) Does anybody in this family realize it's two-fifteen in the morning? (ROY *runs down the corridor to his Father.*)

ROY. Mother's terribly upset about something. (MARY AGNES *is groping under* JAMIE'S *bed.*)

MARY AGNES. I feel like throwing another shoe.

JAMIE. It won't help, Mama—the Bodwells already know. (CHARLEY *weaves sleepily down the corridor.*)

CHARLEY. What's everybody doing up? (*He looks at* JAMIE.) You don't have any clothes on. (JAMIE *has given up explaining.*)

JAMIE. I know.

MRS. BODWELL'S VOICE. (*Off.*) They're coming! They're coming!

CHARLEY. Who's coming?

MARY AGNES. The police. Who did you expect?

CHARLEY. What the hell do we need the police for?

HERMAN. To get the ghost.

MARY AGNES. Now the most important thing for everybody to remember is to keep completely calm, sane, and in control of themselves. Charley, I don't want you to get hysterical.

CHARLEY. When was the last time you saw me hysterical?

MR. BODWELL'S VOICE. (*Off. Hoarse, incoherent.*) Burglars! Burglars! Burglars!

MARY AGNES. (*Clinically.*) I think poor Mr. Bodwell's having an attack again.

JAMIE. (*Thoughtfully.*) Almost everybody we ever lived next to gets attacks.

MARY AGNES. (*Innocently.*) Why do you suppose that is?

ROY. Papa, have you got a gun?

MARY AGNES. A gun? In this house? Your Grandfather'd start the Civil War all over again! (*All eyes drift up toward the attic, where* GRANDPA *sleeps peacefully. There is a mutual sigh of relief that the old man is still asleep.*)

HERMAN. Hey! Listen! (*There is an approaching police-siren. Headlights fan the house as a squad-car screeches to a stop. Police whistles pierce the air.*)

SERGEANT. Okay, men—surround the joint! (MARY AGNES *is delighted with the excitement.*)

MARY AGNES. Jamie, comb your hair. (*Obediently,* JAMIE *runs his fingers through his mop. Three Policemen and a Reporter come on. Each policeman has a flashlight and a drawn gun. The reporter has a drawn note-pad. The cops scatter across the thrust, creep up on the house. The flashlight beams criss-cross nervously, probing for prowlers. The Thurbers huddle dazedly in the upstairs corridor. The police sergeant tries the locked front door,*

*then rings the twisting bell. Another cop rattles the back
screen-door, which is latched.*)

SERGEANT. Open up! Men from Headquarters!

JAMIE. I'll go down and let 'em in.

MARY AGNES. (*Stopping him.*) You haven't a stitch
on.

CHARLEY. (*Bewildered.*) Why did you call the police?

MARY AGNES. Oh, I didn't call them. The Bodwells
did. (*The Police are pounding at the door, getting ready
to smash it in.*)

CHARLEY. Then why aren't they banging on the Bodwells?

MARY AGNES. They usually go where the burglar is.

HERMAN. Or the ghost.

CHARLEY. I don't mind confusion if I know what I'm
confused about.

ROY. (*Craning out the back window.*) There's one in
back, too!

CHARLEY. We'd better let 'em in or they'll break down
the door.

SERGEANT. Break down the door! (*Sergeant and 2nd
policeman put their shoulders to the heavy oak door.
There is the rending of wood, the splatter of glass on the
floor of the entry hall. Their lights play all over the living room. The 2nd cop lets in the 3rd cop* [JOE] *through
the screen door. They race about, stabbing into every
crevice. The family huddles in the hallway.* GRANDPA
*sleeps like a baby in the attic. The reporter comes in the
fractured front door. The sergeant hits him with his
light.*) Who are you?

REPORTER. (*Easily.*) Columbus *Dispatch.* I rode over
with ya! (*The 2nd cop finds* MARY AGNES' *slipper on
the kitchen floor where she threw it.*)

2ND COP. Hey, here's a clue! (*He holds up the slipper.
All lights converge on it.*) A woman's slipper!

SERGEANT. Men! Look for a female cat burglar—half
barefoot!

JAMIE. (*Coming down the stairs.*) No, that's just my

mother's— (*All wheel on* JAMIE *and cover him with their guns and flashlights.*)

SERGEANT. Who are you?

JAMIE. I live here.

SERGEANT. Whassa matta? Ya hot?

MARY AGNES. Jamie, put on some trousers. (*He goes to his room.* MARY AGNES *comes down the front stairs in the manner of a hostess receiving guests at a party.*) Officer, I'm so glad you could come. You and your friends. (*The sergeant looks at her suspiciously. Is she the cat burglar?* ROY *and* HERMAN *come down the stairs behind their Mother.* CHARLEY *comes down in his night-shirt.*)

CHARLEY. Sergeant, I'm sure this can all be very easily explained—but not by me. (*Cops charge up and down the stairs, checking doors, windows, behind and beneath furniture.* HERMAN *sees the milk* CHARLEY *spilled on the kitchen table.*)

HERMAN. He-e-ey . . . ! (*Points at the pool of milk.*) Ghost-blood!

MARY AGNES. (*Calmly.*) It's called "ectoplasm." (HERMAN *backs away, awed.*)

SERGEANT. (*To* MARY AGNES.) No sign of nobody, lady. Musta got away. What'd he look like?

MARY AGNES. (*With dead certainty.*) There were two or three of them. Whooping and carrying on and slamming doors.

SERGEANT. Funny. All ya windows and doors was locked on the inside tight as a tick.

2ND COP. (*To* CHARLEY.) *You* live here?

CHARLEY. Occasionally. (DORA GEDD, *the maid, comes drowsily out of her room into the Kitchen. The police pounce on her. She gives a little scream.*)

SERGEANT. Who're you?

DORA. I'm Dora. I'm the maid. I dint do nuthin'!

MARY AGNES. That's the truth. She didn't even dust.

SERGEANT. Keep an eye on her, Joe; this could be an *inside* job. (*As the policeman moves toward* DORA, *she*

runs off, whimpering—and slams the door behind her.
JAMIE *comes down the back stairs, wearing trousers.*)

JOE. (*Spotting something interesting.*) Lookee here,
Sarge. Here's something suspicious. (*It is a zither. He
strums it with a big paw. It is wildly out-of-tune. The
sergeant takes the zither, turns it over.*)

SERGEANT. Okay, what is it?

JAMIE. It's just an old zither.

ROY. I won it in a pool tournament.

SERGEANT. What's it *for?*

JAMIE. It's not for anything. Our guinea pig used to
sleep on it. (*He gives a penetrating look at* JAMIE, *then
the sergeant turns to* MARY AGNES.)

SERGEANT. That ain't normal.

MARY AGNES. (*Plunking the zither.*) Why not, officer?
It's quite true. Our guinea pig would never sleep anyplace except on Roy's zither. It's a wonder the burglars
didn't take it. (*The three cops and the reporter look from
one to another.*)

REPORTER. There may be a story here—but I don't
think my paper'll print it.

SERGEANT. (*Checking his notebook.*) No sign of
nuthin'. This guy was nekkid. The lady seems historical.
And the head of the house— (*He looks at* CHARLEY, *who
is dozing vertically.*) Hey, fella. (*He pokes at* CHARLEY,
whose head falls.) He just went to sleep standin' up!
(*Makes a note.*) C'mon, let's get outa here. (*Just as they
are starting out,* GRANDPA *rolls over and a saber clanks
onto the Attic floor. The cops look up, excitedly.*) Whas-
sat???!

MARY AGNES. Oh, dear . . . (*They bolt for the attic.
Two go up the front stairs, sergeant goes up the back.
The family protests.*) Just a minute! Officer! Sergeant!
It isn't a good idea to break in on Grandpa unannounced!
Or even announced—! (*But they are banging on the Attic
door, then charging into* GRANDPA'S *sanctum with drawn
guns.*)

GRANDPA.   (*Waking.*)   What   in   thunderation—?

(GRANDPA, *with remarkable spryness for 77 years, leaps up in his nightshirt.*)

SERGEANT. Who're you—?

GRANDPA. I know who you are! Deserters from the Grand Army of the Potomac!

JAMIE. (*Calls.*) Grandpa—!

MARY AGNES. It's just the police—

GRANDPA. Back! Back to the lines, ye cowardly dogs! (*He gropes for his saber.*) There's Rebel cannon-fire to be faced—!

SERGEANT. Let's go boys . . . (*But as the police beat a retreat from the old man, they are piled up in the bottle-neck of the Attic door—and the family, crowding the corridor, also impedes the flight of the cops. Everybody is talking but* GRANDPA's *Philippic roars above everything.*)

GRANDPA. Ye'll not hide out in this attic, ya God-damn lily-livered cattle!!!

2ND POLICEMAN. (*Frightened.*) I'm new on the force— (GRANDPA *pulls the gun out of his hand, brandishing it wildly.*)

SERGEANT. (*With a futile grasp for the gun.*) Fella, yer resisting— (GRANDPA *fires the pistol. The shot cracks the rafters, fills the Attic with smoke. There are cries. The 2nd policeman's shoulder is bleeding. Utter confusion and chaos.*)

MARY AGNES. (*Throwing her arms around* JAMIE.) My God, they've shot your grandfather! (GRANDPA, *delighted with the noise, fires several more shots through the roof.*)

JAMIE. (*Calling.*) Grandpa! Hold your fire! (*The cops are tumbling out of the Attic, carrying the wounded policeman.*)

GRANDPA. Back to the lines! Back! Back! (*From next door, the unseen* MR. BODWELL *is gurgling with dismayed distress.*)

MRS. BODWELL'S VOICE. (*Off.*) We'll go back to Peoria, Merle, and get out of this awful neighborhood! (MRS.

BODWELL'S *voice somehow cuts through the din within the Thurber household. The reporter, marveling, has remained at the foot of the front stairs.* AUNT ESTHER *is still immobile in the oval picture frame in the Entry Hall.* JOE *is examining the 2nd policeman's bleeding shoulder.*)

2ND POLICEMAN. (*Whimpering.*) Don't let 'em amputate—!

JOE. Hardly broke the skin. The old geezer's a pretty good shot: he coulda killed ya!

JAMIE. He thinks you're deserters.

SERGEANT. I'll say he does.

JOE. I'm gonna get my gun back from that old bird.

SERGEANT. Yeah. You and who else?

JAMIE. I'll bring it back to the station house tomorrow. (GRANDPA, *in the attic, is very satisfied with himself; buckles on his saber and dons his Federal soldier's cap— still wearing his night-shirt. The* COPS *carry off their companion, happy to be out of the place.*)

DORA. Mrs. Thurber—? (DORA *stomps into the front room to confront the Thurbers.* DORA *wears a thin cloth coat with a parenthesis of fur at the collar. She carries a suitcase, a corset dangling from it.*) Mrs. Thurber, I am leaving your employment.

MARY AGNES. Why, Dora—whatever for? We've been very happy with your work . . . I mean, at least, you're *clean.*

DORA. I worked for three weeks as a helper to a practical nurse in the Toledo Asylum for the Incurable Insane. But that was the Front Door of Heaven compared with what goes on in this madhouse.

CHARLEY. What about notice—?

DORA. You've got it. (*She goes out the front door into the night, storming past the reporter who has lingered in the Entry Hall. He waggles his fingers in a farewell.*)

JAMIE. (*Calling.*) G'bye, Dora . . . ! (*She is gone. But the reporter stays on—almost like a member of the family.*)

MARY AGNES. Well, that certainly is a peculiar way for

a maid to behave. But we mustn't hold it against her, family. After all, since she's worked in that Toledo crazy house, we can't expect her to be completely normal. Besides, she *never* emptied the water under the ice-box. (*Brightly.*) Well, why don't we all get back to bed? (*Nodding to the reporter, pleasantly.*) Good night. (*They file off up the stairs.* CHARLEY *looks at the splattered glass and the broken door.*)

CHARLEY. (*Shaking his head.*) Keepers of the Peace! (*He goes up the stairs.* JAMIE *starts to exit through the kitchen.*)

REPORTER. (*Gesturing to* JAMIE.) Hey, Bud. Tell me. What the hell is the real lowdown here?

JAMIE. (*Thinks.*) Well-l-l . . . (*He decides to be truthful.*) We had ghosts.

REPORTER. (*Pause.*) Yeah. (JAMIE *goes upstairs to his room. The reporter looks dazed.*) They're all crazy . . . ! The whole bunch of 'em. (*The sepia light rises on* AUNT ESTHER *in the frame, who corrects him.*)

AUNT ESTHER. Not all, young man. (*The reporter jumps as the portrait speaks to him. Where did that voice come from?*) The *Fishers* are sound as clockwork. It's the *Thurber* blood that's tainted: they're nutty as coot-hens! (*But when the reporter looks at the oval frame, the portrait has again become immobile.* GRANDPA *comes down the stairs, whistling.*)

REPORTER. Would you give me your name, sir . . . ?

GRANDPA. (*Sizing him up.*) I'll think about it. F-I-S-H-E-R. Fisher! Care to join me in a bowl of Post Toasties? (*The reporter doesn't. He hurries out the shattered front door.* AUNT ESTHER, *in the picture frame, comes alive again.*)

AUNT ESTHER. Goodbye, young man. (GRANDPA *looks in the ice-box, inspects the empty bottle of milk—and sees the milk spilled on the table.*)

GRANDPA. Who the Sam Hill spilled all the milk?

AUNT ESTHER. The ghost.

GRANDPA. (*Satisfied.*) Oh. (*He sops up the milk with a dish-towel, and starts crunching noisily on a bowl of dry corn flakes.* JAMIE *has put on a shirt and comes warily down the back stairs.* GRANDPA *sees him.*) Howdy, Jamie! Up early, ain't ya?

JAMIE. (*Thinks.*) Uhhh . . . yeah.

GRANDPA. (*Munching away, completely lucid.*) Say, what was the idee of all them cops tarryhootin' 'round the house?

JAMIE. But Grandpa—I thought *you* thought—

GRANDPA. Thought what?

JAMIE. (*Starts back up the stairs.*) Nothing. (*Turns.*) Grandpa, can I ask you a question—?

GRANDPA. Shoot!

JAMIE. What *year* do you think this is?

GRANDPA. Boy, if you don't even know what year it is, you're in trouble! (*Sings.*) "From Atlanta to the sea, while we were marching through Georgia!" (*THE LIGHTS FADE. Immediately, the* GET-READY MAN *calls.*)

VOICE OF GET-READY MAN. (*From* L. *in dark.*) The Worr-ll-d is coming to an end!!! (JAMIE *and* GRANDPA *clear in black.*)

GET-READY MAN. Get ready! Get ready-y . . . ! (*Sunny outdoor light comes up on the thrust as the* GET-READY MAN *pedals on. He rides a flame-red bicycle; a lank unkempt character with wild eyes and a red megaphone.*) Get ready—yyy! The *WOR-LL-D* is COMING TO AN END! (*His bicycle wobbles around the thrust.*) The WURRRRRR-ULD is COMING TO AN END! (*The lights rise on the Kitchen.* MARY AGNES *is framed in the Kitchen window, looking front. The water is running and she is scouring pans. She wears a house-dress and apron. A* CARPENTER *is fixing the front door.*)

MARY AGNES. Of course the world is coming to an end. I don't know why he keeps making such a fuss about it. When it happens, we'll know. (*The* CARPENTER *nods and goes off.*)

GET-READY MAN. Get ready . . . ! Get ready . . . ! (*He rides off on his bicycle.* ROY *clatters downstairs in knickers and a stretched-out sweater.*)

Roy. What was all that?

Mary Agnes. (*Calmly.*) Just the Get-Ready Man.

Roy. Oh. (*Glancing at sink.*) When are we gonna get a new maid, Mama?

Mary Agnes. Roy, we don't have "maids." We just hire guests once in awhile to come in and break a few things. (*Brightly.*) We're interviewing ladies this afternoon.

Roy. This time, let's get one that has teeth, huh? (*Roy darts out the back door, slamming the screen.*)

Mary Agnes. Where you going, Roy?

Roy. I don't have the slightest idea. (*He dashes off. From the dark of the auditorium comes the voice of* Doc Marlowe, *the pitch-man supreme.*)

Doc. Hey, boy-gie! Hey, girl-ie! The Far West has come East to bring you the miracle of the century. (*Doc climbs up onto the thrust. He is a moth-eaten version of General Custer or Buffalo Bill—long hair, drooping mustaches, ten gallon hat with kitchen matches tucked in the band, scarred leggings and a bright colored bead vest. He totes a battered sample case, emblazoned with:* DOC MARLOWE. *He cocks his foot up on the case, leans forward on his knee toward the audience.*) Now, you're wonderin' what's inside this case. (*He scrutinizes various members of the audience. Abruptly, he picks up the case and starts off.*) I don't think I'll tell ya. (*Then, as if swept by a wave of compassion.*) No-o-o, I can't be that cruel. Undoubtedly you noticed this scar on the side of this here case? Was made by the arrow of a *Ho*-pye Indian—a pore ignorant savage who did not know what you intelligent, civilized people are about to find out—that within this box— (*Dramatically, he swings up the lid of the case, revealing lines of medicine bottles. Then he unrolls a chart of the human form in livid colors and with bold labels which indicate the seats of various disorders: Dyspepsia, Insomnia, Dropsy, Gout, Backache, Constipation, Palsy, Fibulation, Twitching, Obesity. He hooks up the chart on an extension of the case. During this, he chants a well-rehearsed pitch.*) It's not the Mohawk ointment; it's not the Black Foot ointment; it's the BLACK HAWK OINT-MENT—from the *Ho*-pye Indians! (JAMIE *has come on, carrying a paper bag. He watches* DOC *with fascination.*) I myself discovered this incredible remedy after I had killed an Indian Chief named Yellow Hand in a toma-hawk duel on horseback. I did not realize that I myself lay mortally wounded. But a friendly savage soothed my flesh with a single drop of this magic ointment. And Glory be to God, I sprang back to full health and the majestic height of manhood that you see before you! (*The* GET-READY MAN *rides across up-stage on his bicycle.*)

GET-READY MAN. Get ready . . . ! Get ready for the end of the worrr-llll-ddd! (DOC *offers the* GET-READY MAN *a bottle, but the* GET-READY MAN *shakes his head "NO" emphatically.*)

DOC. He'll die young. (*Turning back to the audience.*) Now I know you're intelligent people. You've heard about medicine men who try to sell you some cure-all made outa river water. (*Uncapping the bottle.*) But find me a river that smells like *this!* (*He whiffs it ecstatically. Then turns to* JAMIE.) *You* try it, boy. (JAMIE *sniffs.*) That one whiff was lengthened your life as much as 3 months. What do you think?

JAMIE. (*Thinks.*) It's very authentic. (*Within the house,* HERMAN *appears at the top of the back stairs. He wears baseball pants and an undershirt.*)

HERMAN. (*Calling.*) Hey, Ma, where's my baseball shirt?

MARY AGNES. I gave it to Dora to put in the wash. And we never saw it again. (HERMAN, *discouraged, plods down the stairs.*)

HERMAN. Nobody'll know what team I'm on. They'll think I'm something gruesome, like an umpire. (*He galumphs out the back door, also slamming it.* MARY AGNES *winces at the repetition of the sound. She sighs, wraps a towel around her head and goes out into the backyard. From the thrust area,* DOC *singles out a specific woman in the audience.*)

DOC. Madame! (*Pointing directly at her.*) Do you

suffer from pains below the belly button? I am too discreet to name a specific area. The healing properties of this amazing ointment—at the incredibly low price of 35¢ the bottle—will eradicate any ache, discomfiture, ague, crotchet, phelgm, or discombobulation. (*Wheeling quickly to a man in another part of the audience.*) Sir! If you have over-indulged—I am too much of a gentleman to mention what you may have over-indulged in— if you have lost the muscular prowess of your good right arm—or the prowess of some *other* organ—again, I decline to specify—the touch of the liquid gold of the Black Hawk Ointment will restore youth, normalcy, vigor —and that which you thought had declined in force will regain the energy of a schoolboy. What fertilizer is to flowers, my friends, Black Hawk Ointment is to homo sapiens. (GEORGIANA LITTLEFIELD *comes on, eating an ice-cream cone. She is a very attractive girl, a little older than* JAMIE: *she's a Freshman at O.S.U. She crosses directly in front of* DOC, *eating the ice-cream cone sensuously. She looks skeptically at a bottle.*)

GEORGIANA. What's in it?

DOC. Is isn't what's in it, girl-ie; it's what it does! (JAMIE'S *attention responds to glandular programming and shifts from the man with a bottle to the girl with the ice-cream cone.*)

GEORGIANA. What kinda doctor are you?

DOC. What kinda doctor d'ya need? My curative talents are mightily flexible.

JAMIE. I'll take a bottle.

DOC. Sold to the young man with the glow of intelligence in his countenance. Thirty-five cents. (GEORGIANA *crosses* JAMIE *disdainfully.*)

GEORGIANA. You're a shill.

JAMIE. I am not a shill! What's a shill?

DOC. Boy-gie, if you will state the area of your affliction, I will uncork this balm of Gilead and demonstrate here and now the efficacy of—

JAMIE. Oh, it's not for me. It's for my Grandfather.

Doc. What's his trouble?

Jamie. Just about everything.

Doc. Tell you what I'll do. I'll flip ya for it. Double-or nothing! (*He draws a quarter out of his pocket, hands it to* Jamie, *who flips it.*) Heads!

Jamie. (*Uncovering the quarter.*) It's heads. (*Hands back the quarter, then digs in his pocket.*) I don't think I have 70¢.

Doc. (*Patting the boy's shoulder.*) I wouldn't charge double to a friend. (Jamie *gives* Doc *35¢ in nickels.* Doc *gives hims the bottle.*)

Georgiana. (*Licking her cone.*) You could get a week of ice-cream cones for that.

Doc. Who else has the wisdom of this young sage? You, young lady?

Georgiana. (*Coming up to him.*) You oughta be ashamed of yourself! Cheating that dumb kid out of 35¢.

Jamie. Who's a dumb kid?

Georgiana. My Father says anybody who'd buy anything from a con man on a street corner is a moron.

Jamie. He's not a con man! He's a great Western hero. He's practically Buffalo Bill. Besides, what does your Father know?

Georgiana. My Father knows just about everything. He's a *General.* (*With a burst of compassion,* Doc *offers a bottle to* Georgiana.)

Doc. Take him a bottle of this. Being a General is the deadliest disease known to man! (Georgiana *refuses the bottle indignantly.* Doc *shrugs, folds up his case, chanting his pitch as the case collapses magically.*) It's not the Mohawk ointment; it's not the Black Foot ointment; it's the BLACK HAWK OINTMENT—from the *Ho*-pye Indians! (Doc *spots a potential customer off-stage, and starts toward him, calling.* Jamie *and* Georgiana *watch.*) Hey, Boy-gie! What's your trouble—baldness or bunions? Here's the cure. (*Waving a bottle,* Doc *goes off* L. Georgiana *starts to move off* R., *but* Jamie *pursues her.*)

Jamie. You were kidding, weren't you?

GEORGIANA. About what?

JAMIE. Your Father isn't really a General, is he?

GEORGIANA. He sure is.

JAMIE. I didn't know we had one in Columbus. Your name isn't Pershing, is it?

GEORGIANA. (*Loftily.*) Littlefield. My Father is General Littlefield, Commandant of the R.O.T.C. at Ohio State University.

JAMIE. (*Impressed.*) Gosh!

GEORGIANA. But we're hardly any different from ordinary people. I mean, my Father can't help it that he's a distinguished General.

JAMIE. Oh, I wouldn't blame him for a minute.

GEORGIANA. You aren't even in college yet, are you?

JAMIE. I will be next fall. At O.S.U.

GEORGIANA. Then you'll be serving under my Father.

JAMIE. Yeah. (*Uncertainly.*) I'll be looking forward to that.

GEORGIANA. Well, g'bye. (GEORGIANA *starts off* R., JAMIE *wants to keep the conversation going.*)

JAMIE. H-how does a person get to be a General?

GEORGIANA. You have to be a Colonel. And then wait.

JAMIE. How did he get to be a Colonel?

GEORGIANA. I don't know. That was in Perth Amboy.

JAMIE. Perth what?

GEORGIANA. Amboy. In New Jersey. Where I was born. He was a Colonel in the National Guard.

JAMIE. You were actually born in Perth—?

GEORGIANA. Amboy. Then we came out here to the Wild West.

JAMIE. Columbus????? (*The conversation seems to have run out. She starts to go. But he stops her.*) Miss Littlefield— (*She turns.* JAMIE *has a spasm of irrational courage.*) Could I—uh—see you sometime? (GEORGIANA *appraises his face.*)

GEORGIANA. What do you look like without glasses?

JAMIE. I'm not sure. When I don't have glasses on, I can't see myself. (*Gamely.*) If it's important to you, I'll give it a try— (JAMIE *starts to take the glasses off, but she stops him.*)

GEORGIANA. No. It's just that you look a little like Woodrow Wilson. And we're Republicans. (JAMIE *looks dejected.*) But you can call me, if you want to. We're in the Columbus phone book. Well, g'bye! (*She starts to leave.*)

JAMIE. Hey—there may be a lot of Littlefields in the phone book.

GEORGIANA. We're Harvey K. My *father* is. My first name's Georgiana.

JAMIE. That's very unusual.

GEORGIANA. The "ee-ana" was sorta tacked on. Daddy was sure I was gonna be a boy. (*Distastefully.*) "George."

JAMIE. I think you made a very good decision. (JAMIE *shifts hands with the paper bag.*)

GEORGIANA. You carry an awfully heavy lunch.

JAMIE. Oh, this isn't my lunch. This is just something I'm taking back to somebody my Grandfather took it away from. (*Reaching in bag.*) Last night, when he shot the Policeman. (JAMIE *pulls out the policeman's gun, pointing it at* GEORGIANA *without malice.* GEORGIANA *screams and runs off.* JAMIE *looks after her wistfully: boy, did I blow that. He dumps the gun and the medicine bottle in the paper sack and trudges off,* L.)

(*The light rises on a beatific and well-bosomed Aunt in the oval picture frame. It is* AUNT BELINDA. *She has been frozen in a photographic pose, but suddenly comes to life.*)

AUNT BELINDA. I am proud to be one of that boy's eleven maternal great-aunts. We are all Methodists. And we all agree on one thing: anytime a youngster breaks out with symptoms of poetry-writin', play-actin', or pitcher-drawin'—you gotta treat it exactly like pimples, hiccups, dandruff or any other anti-social disease. However, in Jamie Thurber's case, I will blink— (*She blinks.*) —since I am the heroine of the first poem he ever wrote, entitled: "My-Aunt-Mrs.-John-T.-Savage's-Garden-at-185-South-Fifth-Street-Columbus-Ohio."   My goodness, that boy has talent—even if the poem is slightly shorter than the title! (*The light dips on the oval frame.* AUNT BELINDA *assumes the formal pose of a portrait again.* MARY AGNES *struggles in through the back screen-door, lugging a heavy laundry basket piled with clothes she has just taken from the line. She has a maneuver the screen-door open with her hip. A* MRS. WEIR *enters from* R. *and climbs the front stoop. She twists the doorbell with a grandiloquent air.* MRS. WEIR *carries herself like a lady-in-waiting to Queen Victoria. She wears a skimpy fox fur-piece about her neck, one of those things where the fox bites its own tail. She has a wedding-cake hat—without candles.* MARY AGNES *is less than delighted at the sound of the doorbell. She can't find a place to put down the bulging basket in the kitchen, so she goes with it to the door—which she opens with difficulty.*)

MARY AGNES. Yes?

MRS. WEIR. I am here to interview the lady of the house. Would you call her, please? (*She pushes past* MARY AGNES.) Mrs. Thurber is expecting me.

MARY AGNES. (*Blankly.*) She is? (AUNT BELINDA, *in the picture frame, turns to look at the visitor over her shoulder.*)

AUNT BELINDA. (*Distastefully.*) Humph! (AUNT BELINDA *becomes a portrait again.* MRS. WEIR *cruises into the Living Room and sits elegantly in the best chair. She sizes up the room with a sniff.* MARY AGNES, *still carrying the laundry basket and with the towel still about her head, watches the visitor, slightly agape.*)

MRS. WEIR. You may tell her that Elvira Weir is here. I prefer to be called *Mrs.* Weir. (MRS. WEIR *notices Herman's baseball glove on the floor.*) Oh, dear. There are children. How many? (MARY AGNES *puts down the laundry basket and starts to fold clothes, placing them in*

*neat piles around the Living Room. She hauls out first
a pair of* GRANDPA'S *long-johns.*)

MARY AGNES. Scads.

MRS. WEIR. Ages?

MARY AGNES. 14 to 77.

MRS. WEIR. (*Confidentially.*) Tell me, my dear—just
between the two of us—why are you leaving?

MARY AGNES. I'll bet you're answering that ad in
yesterday's paper. For a new maid.

MRS. WEIR. I'm not a "maid." I think of myself more
as a . . . "household coordinator."

MARY AGNES. Ohhh, this is the place for you! If there
was ever a house that needs coordinating—!

MRS. WEIR. I don't do laundry.

MARY AGNES. Mrs. Thurber'll be happy to hear that.

MRS. WEIR. (*Warily.*) And I'll have to interview the
entire family before I agree to stay.

MARY AGNES. I should've done the same thing. (MARY
AGNES *decides to play the role of the departing maid to
the hilt.*) Oh, you'll just love it here. The Thurbers are
divine people. And they can't help it if they're a little
bit—

MRS. WEIR. A little bit what? (JAMIE, *still dejected,
has entered the kitchen and is listening.*)

MARY AGNES. (*Crossing to the dictionary.*) It's hard
to put your finger on the exact word . . . ! (*She riffles
the dictionary.*) I'm not sure it's been invented yet.

MRS. WEIR. How many days a week do they give you
off? (MARY AGNES *breaks into a peal of incredulous
laughter.*)

MARY AGNES. (*Gaily.*) Days off!!!???

MRS. WEIR. Do they give you Thursdays?

MARY AGNES. Right in the teeth.

MRS. WEIR. I'm High Episcopal. That means two ser-
vices every Sunday.

MARY AGNES. Well, if Mrs. Thurber's in a good mood,
she'll let you sneak in the Lord's Prayer over the ironing
board. (*In the kitchen,* JAMIE *opens the ice-box, gets a*

loaf of bread and a paraffin-topped jar of jam. He cuts a ragged slice from the loaf and makes a messy fold-over sandwich. This action continues behind MARY AGNES *and* MRS. WEIR *in the Living Room.*)

MRS. WEIR. (*Stands.*) Well, I—

MARY AGNES. (*With a little gasp.*) Oh, I'm giving you the wrong impression! I don't often have the opportunity to say this, the way they run me ragged around here, but Mrs. Thurber is an absolute angel. Especially when she's asleep. Which in this house isn't very often at night. (*Cheerfully.*) Well, I'll go call her. You can see for yourself. (*But* MARY AGNES *checks herself on the stairs.*) Oh—it may be too early. She sleeps like a floozie all day long. Which will be nice for you, because then she won't keep screaming at you. Unless it's to send you out for a bottle. (MRS. WEIR *is flexed for a fast exit. But* MARY AGNES *blithely pushes her back into the chair.*) Sit *down,* Mrs. Weir! Make yourself comfortable! (MRS. WEIR *looks trapped.* JAMIE *wants to get a peek at what's going on. His Mother sees him, crosses to him and curtsies elaborately.*) Oh, Master Jamie! (*She suddenly goes Irish.*) You'll be after wantin' to meet the new maid. (JAMIE *looks at his Mother gravely, munching on the jam sandwich, then studies* MRS. WEIR *through his thick-lensed glasses.*) Master Jamie's a fine broth of a lad. Upstanding. Considering he was born out of wedlock. (MRS. WEIR *is startled.*) It's all right. He knows. (GRANDPA *starts down the stairs. Her Irish vanishes.*) And this is the distinguished patriarch of the family, Grandfather Fisher. Deaf as a tree stump—but that's the only part of his body that's failing.

GRANDPA. (*Shouting, playing along.*) How's that? What you say?

MARY AGNES. Keep a fair distance from him, dearie! I wouldn't go so far as to say he's a sex maniac— (MRS. WEIR *shrinks back, appalled.*)

GRANDPA. Whad ya say, honey-girl???

MARY AGNES. (*Shouting.*) I said you were a sex maniac!

GRANDPA. (*Slapping* MARY AGNES' *bottom.*) Thanks, baby! The same to you!

MARY AGNES. You never can tell what Grandpa will do when he spots a sweet young girl with a pretty face . . . ! (GRANDPA *suddenly hears.*)

GRANDPA. Pretty face? Young girl? Where? Where? (*He spies* MRS. WEIR *and starts to chase her around the room. Horrified, she flees the Thurber menage forever.* GRANDPA *watches her from the front stoop.*) Lookit her go! Like a dose o'salts through a widow-woman!

JAMIE. She's about the quickest maid we ever had.

MARY AGNES. Well, she certainly wasn't right for us.

JAMIE. Why didn't you tell her that—straight out?

MARY AGNES. I didn't want to hurt her feelings. (*Pleased,* GRANDPA *crosses into the Kitchen whistling.* JAMIE *shakes his head, staring at his jam sandwich.* GRANDPA *is ranging about the Kitchen.*)

GRANDPA. (*Impatiently.*) Some damn fool hid the Post Toasties! (MARY AGNES *crosses into the Kitchen, finds the box of corn flakes under the sink and pours a bowl for* GRANDPA, *who sits down to eat it.* JAMIE *follows her into the Kitchen.*)

JAMIE. Mama . . . Is our whole family Republican?

MARY AGNES. Do you know anybody in Ohio who isn't?

JAMIE. But Dad voted for Teddy Roosevelt. And he's a Bull Moose.

MARY AGNES. *Now* he is. Mr. Roosevelt used to be a Republican, but they got rid of him.

JAMIE. Why?

MARY AGNES. I think he had too many ideas. (*She opens the ice-box and takes out a milk-bottle for* GRANDPA's *cereal. She also lifts out* HERMAN's *baseball shirt.*) Now who in their right mind would put a boy's baseball shirt in the ice-box? (*She smells it; it's pretty gamey.*) Well, maybe there's some logic in it. (*She tosses*

the shirt back in the ice-box. JAMIE *sits, facing his*
GRANDPA *at the Kitchen table.*)

JAMIE. I may not go to college.

GRANDPA. (*Mouth full of corn flakes.*) Good decision.
Waste of time.

MARY AGNES. (*With flat certainty.*) You're going to
college.

JAMIE. Why?

MARY AGNES. For one thing, because I didn't. And
your Father didn't. And a lot of things come up that I
wish I knew more about, and I don't. But *you're* going to
know!

JAMIE. Why don't *you* go to college, Mama? (*This
thought has never really occurred to her.*)

MARY AGNES. Maybe I will. After your Grandfather
grows up. Empty the drip-pan from under the ice-box,
will you, dear? (JAMIE *does, thoughtfully; they talk
through the action.*) I want you to be prepared.

JAMIE. For what? I don't even know how to talk to a
girl.

MARY AGNES. College'll teach you.

JAMIE. They have courses in that?

MARY AGNES. I think it comes up in biology.

GRANDPA. Is she pretty?

JAMIE. Is who pretty?

GRANDPA. This girl you're not goin' to college so's you
can talk to.

JAMIE. Oh. *That* girl. (*Self-consciously.*) She was just
somebody walking down the street sort of kissing an ice-
cream cone.

MARY AGNES. That sounds interesting.

JAMIE. She isn't a native.

MARY AGNES. That wouldn't matter—we're not prejudiced.

JAMIE. Of Columbus, I mean. She's from— (*He squints,
trying to think of it. He can't.*) —someplace in New
Jersey.

GRANDPA. Well, Ohio ain't everywhere, boy. (*He tilts*

the cereal bowl like a tea-cup, to drain the dregs.) Confederates didn't even take a nibble at it. They had a bigger hankerin' for Pennsylvania.

JAMIE. I didn't even tell her my name.

MARY AGNES. Why not?

JAMIE. I dunno. A sophisticated college girl from the Eastern Seaboard—

MARY AGNES. Kissing ice-cream cones doesn't sound so sophisticated.

JAMIE. When I tell people my name's "Thurber," they always say "What?"

GRANDPA. Don't blame me. I'm a Fisher.

JAMIE. (*Reflectively.*) A Fisher fishes. Maybe a Thurber thurbs. Are we a verb, Mama? I thurb, you thurb, he-she-or-it thurbs.

MARY AGNES. Oh, we're definitely a verb. Active, not passive.

JAMIE. And irregular. (*Sighs.*) I don't know if I can go all through life just *thurbing.*

GRANDPA. Try fishing.

JAMIE. (*Restless.*) Who from Ohio ever really *did* anything?

MARY AGNES. Presidents.

JAMIE. That's what I mean. If Christopher Columbus had been born in Columbus, d'you think he'd ever have discovered Spain?

MARY AGNES. How about the Wright Brothers?

JAMIE. They're from Dayton.

MARY AGNES. It's this town, all right. Something about the air. (JAMIE *is juggling the drip-pan.*) Just pour it down the sink. (JAMIE *does. He and his Mother are facing front, framed by the Kitchen window.*) Columbus is nervous.

JAMIE. How, nervous?

MARY AGNES. Well, your Father was going through a bunch of old papers down at the State House. And he found out that early in eighteen-hundred-something Columbus beat out Lancaster, Ohio, for State Capitol by—

how much do you think? One vote! When it's that close, I guess you can't blame a city if it keeps looking back over its shoulder as if it's being followed. (MARY AGNES *bites a fingernail and looks hunted.* JAMIE *laughs.*)

JAMIE. What if Columbus isn't here at all? Maybe it's just a state of mind.

GRANDPA. (*Delighted.*) The whole damned state of Ohio is a state of mind! If we stop thinking about it, maybe it'll go away. (GRANDPA *meanders into the Living Room and begins setting up checkers on a small table, putting a chair on either side.* MARY AGNES *leans on the sink, dreamily.*)

MARY AGNES. Columbus, Ohio, *could* just be an idea. Not a very good idea, but— (*She puts her arm around the boy.*) —we live here, don't we!

JAMIE. How can you live in an idea?

MARY AGNES. (*Brusquely rumpling his hair.*) Would you rather be a flea and live in a dog's back? (*They laugh. Then* MARY AGNES *is thoughtful.*) I don't see why a person shouldn't live in an idea. As long as it's *his* idea. (*In the Living Room,* GRANDPA *is searching stormily about.*)

GRANDPA. Some damn fool hid my checkers hat! (*From off stage* L. *comes an irregular roaring and chugging, as of an ancient automobile.* MARY AGNES *and* JAMIE *peer out the Kitchen window.*)

JAMIE. (*Astonished.*) Hey! The car actually made it home!

MARY AGNES. Oh? I didn't know it was gone. I never even heard your Father start it up.

JAMIE. (*Patiently.*) Mama, did you *ever* hear the Reo start?

MARY AGNES. It's been years.

JAMIE. D'you suppose we'll ever get a car we don't have to push . . . ?

MARY AGNES. Well, once it starts it's nice. And it's good exercise for you boys. And I *am* partial to those flowers vases in the back seat. (*The sputtering engine subsides with an asthmatic wheeze off stage.*)

GRANDPA. How you 'spect me to play checkers without a hat??? (MARY AGNES *goes to help him find it.* CHARLEY, HERMAN *and* ROY *come up the front stoop, loaded with electrical equipment—a bevy of sockets and great coils of wire. They come into the Living Room.*)

MARY AGNES. What's all that?

CHARLEY. We're going electric. Half the houses on this block have electricity. Why shouldn't we???

ROY. When you've got a light bulb burning a burglar doesn't dare break in.

HERMAN. Or a ghost.

MARY AGNES. Who's going to put all this *in???*

CHARLEY. I am. We are. The boys and I!

HERMAN. Roy read a book. On how to electrocute a house!

MARY AGNES. You're not going to electrocute *my* house!

GRANDPA. (*Stomping about.*) Where the Sam Hill's my checkers hat?

JAMIE. (*Squinting at some of the coiled wire.*) What's all the wire for?

ROY. That's how it works. That's what the electricity pours through.

MARY AGNES. (*Looking at another strand of wire.*) What keeps it *in?* I mean, what keeps it from spilling out? (CHARLEY *has climbed up on a chair and is disconnecting gas mantles.*)

CHARLEY. Just don't you worry, Mary Agnes. The boys and I have got it all figured out. We're just gonna shove these wires through the gas lines and then hook up the bulbs.

MARY AGNES. Oh, God!

GRANDPA. A man can't play checkers without a hat! (MARY AGNES *finds an old visored cap under a sofa pillow, hands it to* GRANDPA, *who ignores the commotion over the electricity, goes to the checkers table.*)

JAMIE. (*Looking out the kitchen window.*) The car's parked pretty far out from the curb.

HERMAN. (*Proudly.*) Yeah. Dad let me steer. I left it like that on purpose. Leaning downhill a little so it'll be easier to push.

MARY AGNES. (*Also looking out the window.*) Charley, the car looks worried.

CHARLEY. (*Preoccupied.*) What?

MARY AGNES. I hope you haven't been driving the Reo all over town without gasoline.

CHARLEY. (*With a short laugh.*) If I could, I would.

MARY AGNES. Oh, you mustn't. It's dangerous to drive an automobile without gasoline. It fries the valves or something.

ROY. (*Calling.*) Jamie, come on and help us with the wiring.

JAMIE. I don't know anything about electricity.

MARY AGNES. Neither do I. (*Warily picking up a wire, then discarding it as if it were a snake.*) And I don't want to have it explained to me.

HERMAN. It all comes from this dynamite down on South High Street—

JAMIE. Dynamo.

HERMAN. I thought you didn't know anything about it. (GRANDPA *addresses the empty chair opposite him.*)

GRANDPA. Red moves first. (*He moves spryly to the other chair and puts the hat on . . . and hereafter 'he wears the hat only while playing from the "red" position.*)

CHARLEY. When we get this rigged up, all they have to do is plug us in! And then—

MARY AGNES. Bang! Not this house you don't plug into any dynamite.

CHARLEY. Now, don't you worry, Mary Agnes.

MARY AGNES. If you're so set on this, why don't we hire somebody who—

CHARLEY. Do you realize those electric workers get as high as 30¢ an hour!?

MARY AGNES. If you've got electricity sneaking all through the walls—

CHARLEY. (*Lifting down a gas mantle.*) We know what we're doing.

JAMIE. Dad. D'ya think ya ought to turn off the gas first? (CHARLEY *pauses, sniffs the escaping gas.*)

CHARLEY. Good idea. (CHARLEY *strides to the front door with* HERMAN, *the tagalong.*)

JAMIE. The gas turn-off is out back. (CHARLEY *is slightly annoyed at* JAMIE's *knowledge. He crosses to go out the back door,* HERMAN *skipping behind him.* GRANDPA *makes a "red" move. Then he pulls the hat off, moves to the other chair.*)

GRANDPA. (*Addressing the empty chair.*) That's a stinkin' first move. (AUNT IDA *has struck a photographic pose in the hallway frame. She is the family Cassandra, in love with disaster.* IDA *surveys the Living Room with dilated doom-filled eyes.*)

MARY AGNES. We got along all these years without electricity. . . .

ROY. Mama, you can have an electric ice-box!

MARY AGNES. And put the ice-man out of business?

JAMIE. We don't use the ice man. Roy's the ice man.

MARY AGNES. (*Crossing to the Kitchen.*) That horse looks so unhappy . . .

ROY. What horse?

MARY AGNES. That pulls the ice-wagon. Whenever I fix myself a glass of lemonade, I think of that poor animal's face, and it spoils it.

ROY. Do you ever think of *my* face? Pulling a 50-pound cake of ice home in Herman's wagon?

MARY AGNES. You're different, Roy. You can complain about it. But that poor horse just *looks*. Besides, the floor of the ice wagon looks dirty.

ROY. Have you ever seen the floor of the ice *house?*

MARY AGNES. No, and don't tell me. (GRANDPA *makes a move, switches chairs, dons the hat.*)

GRANDPA What're you up to, you old coot? (CHARLEY *and* HERMAN *re-enter from the back.*)

CHARLEY. All right, boys. Start the wires through the pipes. (*There is general confusion as they untangle wire and start to feed it through the gas pipe.* GRANDPA *ponders over the checkerboard.* MARY AGNES, *at the sink, wants nothing to do with this new venture.*)

AUNT IDA. When the Throckmortons put in electricity, it was just before they lost all their money. (GRANDPA *switches chairs to become hat-less black.*) And that Sigafoos boy—what was his name?

GRANDPA. (*From the midst of his checker game.*) Ned.

AUNT IDA. Ned Sigafoos. Always puttering around with electricity. He won't live to dance at his own wedding.

GRANDPA. Ned Sigafoos has been married twice and has eight children.

AUNT IDA. Well, that's what electricity can do, if you aren't careful. (HERMAN *is working the wire, which isn't moving.*)

HERMAN. It doesn't want to poke.

ROY. Push harder. You must be at a bend in the pipe. (*A fragile wraith of a maid-applicant knocks at the back door.* MARY AGNES *crosses to open it.*)

MARY AGNES. Yes?

LILY LOOMIS. It's gone, isn't it?

MARY AGNES. Gone?

LILY LOOMIS. (*Tearfully.*) The job. You've already hired somebody. I knew I'd be too late.

MARY AGNES. No, no, come in. (GRANDPA *switches chairs, puts on the hat, scowls at the board.* JAMIE, HERMAN, ROY *and* CHARLEY *are all tugging at the wire.*)

CHARLEY. Damn, damn, double-damn!

AUNT IDA. It'll come to no good—!

LILY LOOMIS. (*Sadly.*) I hope you're a cheerful family. I couldn't work anyplace that wasn't cheerful. (*But* LILY *herself is almost dissolved in tears.*)

MARY AGNES. Do you have any references, Miss—?

LILY LOMMIS. *Mrs.* Loomis. Lily Loomis. *I'm* the only

person I've ever worked for. I never dreamt that after Mr. Loomis passed on I'd have to stoop to— (GRANDPA *lets out a whoop, whips off the hat, switches chairs.*)

GRANDPA. (*Making a triple-jump.*) *Got*cha!!! (*He switches to the other chair, puts the hat back on.*) Oh, ya think so, do ya? (GRANDPA *makes a triple-jump the other way. Chortling:*) You're not so smart! (*Whipping off the hat,* GRANDPA *crosses to the other chair, slumps into it dejectedly. He scratches his head.*) Goddam! I didn't see that. (JAMIE *has lost interest in the increasing tangle of electric wire.*)

JAMIE. Grandpa, when you play checkers with yourself, why do you keep putting on and taking off that hat?

GRANDPA. That's a stupid question, boy. That's how I remember which side I'm on!

HERMAN. Whyn'tcha get somebody else to play against, Grandpa?

GRANDPA. (*Snorts.*) Nobody around here is as good competition as I am. (*Then slyly.*) Besides, I've made a few improvements in the rules!

LILY LOOMIS. I don't know if I could work here. Mr. Loomis and I had a house that was exactly like this—!

MARY AGNES. I doubt if it was *exactly* like this one . . .

LILY LOOMIS. And we used to have an ice-box just like that . . . ! (*She holds back the tears.* MARY AGNES *is sentimental, too.*)

MARY AGNES. So did we.

ROY. Hey, Dad, we got the wire past the kink. It's going through just great now!

CHARLEY. Good boy! (HERMAN *helps as they feed the wire rapidly into the chandelier. What they do not see is that a wire is rising from the front burner of the porcelain stove in the Kitchen.*)

ROY. I'll jiggle it a little to make sure it's clear. (*He works the wire back and forth. The wire erupting from the stove rises and falls synchronously. But nobody in the household sees.*)

HERMAN. Boy, we'll have 'lectric light bulbs burning all over the house by dark! (*As rapidly as they feed it into the wall it curls out of the stove. LILY LOOMIS sees it, freezes, hypnotized, as if by a cobra.*)

CHARLEY. Herman, run down to the gas meter and let us know as soon as the wire gets there.

HERMAN. Yup! (HERMAN *slams out the kitchen door. MARY AGNES watches ROY and CHARLEY skeptically, hands on her hips. She is unaware that the wire is snaking toward her from the kitchen stove.*)

AUNT IDA. (*From her frame.*) If God Almighty had meant man to be electrical, He'd've borned us all with lightning rods on our heads.

GRANDPA. (*Brooding over the checker board.*) Oh, shut up, Ida! (*The wire from the stove has now wriggled up to MARY AGNES and is tickling her back. At first, she tries to brush it off, thinking it's an insect. Then MARY AGNES turns, sees the attacking wire, jumps.*)

MARY AGNES. Stop! Don't you crawl another inch into my house!

CHARLEY. Hold it, Roy. Looks like we caught the wrong bend in the pipe. (HERMAN *runs in through the screen door.*)

HERMAN. Nothing coming out yet, Dad— (*Sees the wire, delighted.*) Hey, we gonna have an electric stove, too???

CHARLEY. Not on purpose. Roy, what did you do with that book of yours? (*From off L. there is the clanging of a street-car, which seems to clatter stereophonically across the auditorium through the following. They all look front —except GRANDPA who is absorbed by his checkerboard and LILY LOOMIS who is immobilized by the trembling wire in the Kitchen.*)

JAMIE. (*Panicky, looking out the Kitchen window.*) Somebody move the Reo. A street-car's coming.

ROY. The motorman'll stop!

MARY AGNES. He never stops—not even for passengers! (MARY AGNES *and* JAMIE *race out the back way,* CHAR-

LEY, ROY *and* HERMAN *seem to leap out the front. They converge on the thrust, waving their arms, shouting.*)

ALL. Stop! Stop!

CHARLEY. (*Calling.*) We'll move it! (*He gropes in his pockets.*) Where's the key????

MARY AGNES. Forget the key—*push!!!!* (MARY AGNES *holds* JAMIE *back as the streetcar grinds and clangs inexorably closer.*)

JAMIE. It's caught in the cow-catcher!

AUNT IDA. (*From her frame, with dire joy.*) Doom! Disaster! *Catastrophe!!! (The five Thurbers watch, horrified—their eyes following the monstrous Jabberwock come to devour their beloved chariot. The cries are simultaneous:*)

CHARLEY. Put on your breaks, you crazy fool . . . !

HERMAN. Don't do that to our Reo . . . !

ROY. Watch out, Mama—stand back . . . ! (*In the face of tumultuous clanging,* MARY AGNES *plunges forward, arms outstretched, as if she were going to throw herself on the tracks.* CHARLEY *and the* BOYS *pull her back. Crunch of metal on metal! A grinding, tearing, laceration of street-car versus Reo!*)

MARY AGNES. (*An anguished cry.*) Ooo-hhhhhhhh—! (*A tremendous crash and a shower of electrical sparks from off* R. *Bolts and gadgets fly onto the thrust as if spinning from a Catharine Wheel. A fender, an agonized headlamp, a 1917 license-plate all clang onto the stage. The Thurbers stand back, awed by the carnage. The steering wheel rolls across the stage with a melancholy whistling sound. A flower vase, miracuolusly intact with one artificial rose, lands at* MARY AGNES' *feet. A tire wobbles on stage, expires with a hissing death. The eyes of the Thurbers have followed the street-car from its approach, Stage Left, to the collision—Center. Now the sound of the street-car travels off Stage Right—and the family continues to watch with unbelieving horror as the old Reo is drubbed unmercifully away. Except for the rem-nants at their feet, the street-car has picked up the tired old automobile like a terrier with a rabbit in its teeth. The sound fades away. The family is stunned.* MARY AGNES— *shouting at the departed streetcar.*) Beast!!! CAR-KILLER!!! Reo-wrecker!

JAMIE. (*Picking up the bent license-plate.*) Our Reo. Born, 19-oh-9. Died, April, 1917. (*In the ozone-charged aftermath, the Thurbers realize the enormity of the tragedy. Silent tears stream down* MARY AGNES' *face.* HERMAN *whimpers.* ROY *has a blurting asthmatic sob.* JAMIE, *disbelieving tears in his eyes, offers* ROY *his handkerchief. In the picture frame,* AUNT IDA *blows her nose noisily.*)

CHARLEY. (*Shaken.*) I useta get sick to my stomach pushing it—but I loved that old wreck! (*A sob breaks through his masculine restraint. This is the cue for everybody to loosen up and have a good cry. Everybody except* LILY LOOMIS *who is still motionless in the Kitchen, hypnotized by the wavering wire; and* GRANDPA, *who has reached the triumphant climax of his checker game. On the hatless black side,* GRANDPA *captures the final red pieces.*)

GRANDPA. (*With a victorious whoop of laughter.*) Finally beat ya, you old bastard! Now get out of the house, you son-of-a-bitch—and take yer hat with ya! (*He strides to the front door and flings the hat contemptuously off-stage after his imaginary opponent.* MARY AGNES *leans down and tenderly picks up the vase.*)

MARY AGNES. (*Sentimentally.*) Nothing left but beauty . . . ! (*Her burst of sobs is infectuous as hiccups. The whole family is now in noisy tears.* GRANDPA *turns sharply at the sound of sorrow.*)

GRANDPA. Who died??? (*This starts another emotional wave.* GRANDPA *comes down the front stoop to the midst of the grief-stricken family.*) Herman! Something happened to Herman! (*Sees* HERMAN.) Oh, hello, Herman. Glad you're still with us. (*Another dire thought.*) It was Roy. Poor Roy—! (*Sees* ROY.) Oh, hullo, Roy. (*Another thought.*) Jamie?

JAMIE. Nobody's dead, Grandpa. (GRANDPA *hugs the boy. Then looks around.*)

GRANDPA. Then what's all the blubberin' about?

MARY AGNES. Pa. The car—

GRANDPA. The what—?

JAMIE. The Reo.

GRANDPA. Who?

MARY AGNES. The automobile. It's all smashed.

GRANDPA. (*Slight pause.*) What's an automobile?

MARY AGNES. (*Turning away, sadly.*) Oh, Pa . . . ! (GRANDPA *turns to* CHARLEY.)

GRANDPA. Now tell me, Charley, man-to-man. Whatcha hidin' from me? Who died?

CHARLEY. Nobody died. There was just this terrible accident—

GRANDPA. I knew it. I knew it. (*Sternly.*) Was he drunk?

CHARLEY. Was who drunk?

GRANDPA. Who d'ya think? *Zenas!* He was drunk, wasn't he?

HERMAN. Who's Zenas?

MARY AGNES. (*Pale.*) Zenas . . . ?

AUNT IDA. (*Urgently.*) Don't tell 'em about Zenas, Mary Agnes! Don't tell, for the honor of the family . . . !

JAMIE. I never heard you say anything about Zenas, Mama.

ROY. Is he a relative?

GRANDPA. You're just puttin' on, tryin' to hide it from me. Well, I know you're all cryin' because Zenas died and you don't want me t'know about it.

CHARLEY. Zenas isn't dead—

GRANDPA. He isn't!?

CHARLEY. Well, yes, he's dead, but—

GRANDPA. Make up yer mind, is he or isn't he?

MARY AGNES. Yes, Pa, Zenas is dead, but that's not what we were crying about.

GRANDPA. When's the funeral?

MARY AGNES. There isn't going to be any funeral.

GRANDPA. There's gotta be a funeral! You can't just leave him lyin' around the house!

JAMIE. (*The peacemaker.*) Don't be so upset, Grandpa . . .

GRANDPA. Upset? Of course I'm upset! When a man's own family don't wanta give his own brother a decent Christian burial. Now I'm not gonna eat so much as one corn-flake until you set the time and the place for the funeral! (GRANDPA *notices his bright-colored suspenders.*) These galluses ain't respectful to Zenas—lyin' there fresh-cold! I gotta put on my black ones. (*He strides up the stoop into the house. As he passes the portrait of Aunt Ida, he says to the picture:*) Ya hear what happened, Ida? Zenas just passed on! Get outa that dancin' costume and put on your best black! (*In the picture frame,* IDA *shakes her head and blows her nose again.* GRANDPA *storms up the stairs to the attic.*)

JAMIE. (*Staring after* GRANDPA.) Mama . . . if Zenas was Grandpa's brother, then he was your uncle. And our *great* uncle. (MARY AGNES *retreats toward the front stoop.*)

MARY AGNES. (*Unwillingly.*) Well, there wasn't anything really "great" about Uncle Zenas.

ROY. Is he alive or dead?

MARY AGNES. Oh, he's dead all right.

HERMAN. When's the funeral?

MARY AGNES. (*Sitting on the top step of the stoop.*) He died in . . . 1866, wasn't it, Charley . . . ?

CHARLEY. (*Charitably.*) Boys, you know how your Grandfather gets a little mixed up on time.

ROY. Well, if he was a member of the family, we've got a right to know who he *was!*

MARY AGNES. (*Setting her mouth firmly.*) Don't ask me about Uncle Zenas. Ask me anything else. Anything you want to know. You want to know about girls? I'll tell you about girls.

ROY. We know about girls.

MARY AGNES. Then I'll tell Herman about girls.

HERMAN. I already know. Roy told me.

JAMIE. We want to hear about Uncle Zenas. (MARY AGNES *takes a deep breath, looks toward her husband.*)

MARY AGNES. Charley . . . ?

CHARLEY. Oh, no. He wasn't a Thurber. He was a Fisher. He's yours! *You* tell 'em! (CHARLEY *moves a little off* R. *as the boys cluster around* MARY AGNES *and probe for information.*)

HERMAN. Did he have a crash? Was he drunk-driving an automobile?

MARY AGNES. No, no . . . the automobile hadn't quite been invented . . . (CHARLEY *crosses his arms impatiently.*)

CHARLEY. For God's sake, *tell* 'em, Mary Agnes! They're old enough to know.

MARY AGNES. (*Taking a deep breath.*) Well—Herman, go get the family album.

HERMAN. Where is it?

MARY AGNES. Under the dictionary. I think. (HERMAN *goes in the house.* AUNT IDA *is panicked in the picture frame.*)

AUNT IDA. No! Don't tell them, Mary Agnes!

MARY AGNES. (*Hedging.*) It's so shameful. (*Bracing herself.*) You see, your Uncle Zenas was—

AUNT IDA. (*Throwing up her hands.*) I can't stand it! I won't listen! (*She turns and flees, leaving the picture frame an empty oval.* HERMAN *has found the photo album, ignores the blank picture frame in the Entry Hall and hands the book to* MARY AGNES, *seated on the front stoop. She takes the album—holds it clamped shut for a moment, dreading what she has to expose.*)

MARY AGNES. I guess every family has its shame . . . (*Reluctantly she opens the album, leafs through it, then points guardedly to a faded daguerreotype almost hidden in the center binding. Sighs:*) *He's* ours.

JAMIE. Is that Uncle Zenas? (MARY AGNES *nods.*)

ROY. Oh, I noticed him in there once. I asked Grandpa who it was, and he just said "Shut up!"

HERMAN. What're all those splotchy things on his face?

MARY AGNES. Well, it could be the photograph. But it isn't. (*She takes a deep breath.*) Of course, I never knew him personally. I just . . . *heard* about him. Nobody ever wanted to talk about Zenas.

ROY. Why not?

MARY AGNES. Well, he wasn't really a *bad* boy.

HERMAN. He was just a horse-thief.

MARY AGNES. (*Looking up to heaven.*) Oh, I wish to God that's all he was! You can see from his face he was the sensitive sort. Poetical, I think. And when the Civil War broke out, Zenas ran off to South America. He wrote one letter back to your Aunt Ida—she burned it—something like: "I'm staying here in Venezuela until the whole mess blows over."

JAMIE. I don't think that's so terrible. He just didn't want to shoot people. Or get shot.

MARY AGNES. Well . . . that's not quite all. (*From R., GEORGIANA comes on. She carries what looks like a chrome miniature of the Winged Victory. MARY AGNES and the boys are so intent on the album and the story they do not notice GEORGIANA. CHARLEY gives a cautionary cough, but they don't hear him.*) A little while after Civil War had "blown over," Zenas came back. And he got sick.

ROY. From what?

MARY AGNES. It's unmentionable . . . !

HERMAN. (*Gleefully.*) Leprosy???

MARY AGNES. (*Shaking her head.*) No other human being ever had it before. Or since. Zenas caught the same disease that was killing off the chestnut trees in those years!

JAMIE. (*Awed.*) How did they know?

MARY AGNES. Well, he had the same kind of spots. And he leaned a little! (*Blurting out the family secret.*) It's the only case in history where a tree doctor had to be called in to spray a *person!* (*GEORGIANA laughs.*)

GEORGIANA. Somebody in your family had the chestnut tree blight? (*The family sees her. MARY AGNES slams the album shut and hides it behind her back.* JAMIE *takes a step toward* GEORGIANA, *then looks embarrassedly back at his family.*)

JAMIE. (*Awkwardly.*) Oh. This is Georgiana. Miss Littlefield (*To* GEORGIANA, *pointing vaguely to the others.*) This is—everybody. My—my family.

GRANDPA. (*Shouting from the attic.*) Who the goddam Sam Hill hid my burying suspenders?

JAMIE. (*In a small voice.*) And that's my grandfather. (GEORGIANA *holds the Winged Victory radiatorcap out toward* JAMIE.)

GEORGIANA. We found this on our front lawn after the street-car went by. And you're the only people I know who have a Reo. I mean that *kind* of Reo.

JAMIE. Yeah.

GEORGIANA. I think this radiator-cap fell off your car.

JAMIE. In a way, the car fell off the radiator-cap. (JAMIE *takes the Winged Victory, then hands it to* MARY AGNES, *who is stuck with it, as if it were some kind of County Fair prize.*) Thanks, Georgiana.

GEORGIANA. You're welcome. (*She starts off, but stops when there is a shout from the attic too fascinating to miss.*)

GRANDPA. (*Bellowing from above.*) Rest easy, Zenas! We're gonna give you a fittin' funeral! And I'm gonna lead the Honor Guard! (*Shouting down still louder.*) Somebody dig up a bugle! We gotta sound taps for that fine boy!

GEORGIANA. Who died?

MARY AGNES. (*Picking up a few assorted nuts and bolts.*) Only our Reo. And there's not much left of that to bury.

CHARLEY. (*Cupping his hands, shouting back to the attic.*) There *isn't* gonna be a funeral, Pa! (*Now* GRANDPA *is in a towering rage.*)

GRANDPA. Put the funeral off any longer, and I'll report it to the Board of Health! (GEORGIANA *drifts back toward the family: she's never seen people behave like this and she's mightily intrigued.* MARY AGNES *and the others lower their voices out of embarrassment with an outsider watching and listening.*)

MARY AGNES. Boys, we've got to set your Grandfather's mind straight. (*A sudden inspiration.*) Maybe if somebody got dressed up and impersonated Uncle Zenas—

ROY. Who could do that?

MARY AGNES. We could hire an actor—!

ROY. There aren't any actors in Columbus.

MARY AGNES. The trouble with your Grandpa isn't what he forgets, it's what he remembers.

JAMIE. When he's fighting the Civil War, it's sorta fun. It's when he gets back to *now* that it kinda gives you a jolt.

MARY AGNES. Boys, we've just go to resurrect Uncle Zenas.

JAMIE. Hey! I know a fella who's more of an actor than an actor. (*JAMIE starts out, then comes back for the photo-album. Points to the picture.*) He even has a mustache like that.

MARY AGNES. Get him! (*JAMIE, album in hand, starts out again, thinks of something, stops.*)

JAMIE. What was Grandpa's first name before everybody called him "Grandpa"?

MARY AGNES. Clem.

JAMIE. Clem???? (*He dashes off. GEORGIANA pases by the family, looks at them strangely, as if they were something in a freak show.*)

GEORGIANA. How can a person catch the chestnut tree blight?

MARY AGNES. (*Weakly.*) Up *our* family tree, *anything* is possible! (*GEORGIANA goes off. MARY AGNES, CHARLEY, ROY and HERMAN shamble back into the house through the Kitchen. In the Attic, GRANDPA has found his black suspenders and is strapping them on. LILY LOOMIS has remained immobile, numb as a pillar of salt through the entire car wreck.*)

CHARLEY. (*To* MARY AGNES.) Is that anybody we know?

MARY AGNES. It's the new maid.

ROY. Is she any good?

MARY AGNES. We're not sure. At least she hasn't broken anything yet.

HERMAN. What's wrong with her?

MARY AGNES. Nothing. I think she's hypnotized. (MARY AGNES *crosses to* LILY LOOMIS, *slaps her face.*)

LILY LOOMIS. (*Snapping out of it.*) Oh! I quit!

MARY AGNES. You can't—we haven't hired you. (LILY LOOMIS *gets another look at the quavering cobra of wire, covers her eyes with a little squeak and runs out the back door.* GRANDPA *has put on a black frock coat. Now he comes down the stairs, trying a black string tie.*) Oh, hello, Pa. You look very nice. (JAMIE *comes up the front stoop,* DOC MARLOWE *in tow.*)

DOC MARLOWE. (*Rehearsing.*) I'm Clem. He's Zenas.

JAMIE. No. You're Zenas, *he's* Clem.

DOC MARLOWE. Gotcha! (JAMIE *flings open the front door, points inside toward* GRANDPA. DOC *makes a cock-sure "leave it to me" gesture, takes a deep breath and sails into the house like a ham-actor making his first entrance. Inside the Living Room,* DOC *throws out his hands expansively.*) Clem!!!!! (GRANDPA *turns slowly, looks at* DOC.)

GRANDPA. Who *air* you?

DOC MARLOWE. I'm Zenas! Your brother Zenas, fit as a fiddle and sound as a dollar! (GRANDPA'S *eyes narrow.*)

GRANDPA. Zenas, my foot. Zenas died of the chestnut blight in '66! (*All are stunned by this flash of lucidity.* GRANDPA *dismisses the imposter with a wave, turns to* MARY AGNES.) Now, what in Sam Hill happened to the goddam Reo?

MARY AGNES. It flew all to pieces, Pa.

GRANDPA. (*With a growl.*) I knew 'twould. I allus told you to git a Pope-Toledo. Now where the hell are the Post Toasties? (DOC *shrugs, starts out of the house.*

JAMIE *follows him to the stoop inside,* MARY AGNES *and* CHARLEY *have coffee, delighted to feed the now-quieted* GRANDPA *his cornflakes.*)

JAMIE. Gee, thanks, Doc. . . . You're a good friend, helping out like that—

DOC. Ya-a-ahhh . . . too bad it didn't work. Guess I'm not a very good actor. Maybe I'm too honest.

JAMIE. Aw, you're better than any actor; they just make up the great things they do . . . you've *done* 'em! (DOC *puts his arm around* JAMIE, *who looks up at him with profound admiration.*)

DOC. Yeah-h-h. Tell ya what we're gonna do. Some day, Boy-gie, we're gonna git ourselves a coupla pinto ponies, and ride ourselves straight west into the sunset! Clean all the way to Comanche country—!!!

JAMIE. (*Impressed.*) He-ey . . .

DOC. Just the two of us. You and me. Wouldja like that?

JAMIE. I've read practically every book about the Wild West I could get my hands on.

DOC. (*Putting his hand on* JAMIE'S *shoulder.*) Boy-gie, book-readin' is like listenin' to a fella tell ya how *he* kissed a pretty girl. It's better when you do it yourself. (*Gesturing broadly toward the sky.*) No book's gonna give ya the feel of the great plains, the dust in your pores, the salt of the mighty Pacific on your lips . . .

JAMIE. I'll go pack!

DOC. Don't you have to go to college?

JAMIE. I'll learn more from you than from any old college. And we gotta go soon, Doc . . . while there's still some Indians left.

DOC. There's enough to last. You go to college, Boy-gie, Meanwhile, we'll make plans. Big plans. 'Cause you and me are gonna see things that'll make them book-writers look like lie-tellers. We're gonna see the AWE-thentic truth! (*Bells begin ringing. Somewhere in the distance a band begins "Tipperary." The* GET-READY MAN *bicycles crazily across the thrust.*)

GET-READY MAN. Get ready! Get ready! THE END OF THE WORRRRRLLLLLD IS HERE!

MARY AGNES. Oh, not today—we don't have time! (*All the family stream out of the house.* DOC MARLOWE, *who has started off, turns back to watch as the big news breaks.*)

GET-READY MAN. Woodrow Wilson has declared war!

ROY. War?

MARY AGNES. Oh, don't listen to him—he's always ending the world!

MR. BODWELL'S VOICE. (*Shouting from next door.*) War! The U.S. is at war!

MRS. BODWELL'S VOICE. (*Off.*) We'll stay out of it, Merle! We'll move back to Peoria!

MARY AGNES. (*Looking at her three sons.*) Oh, God—!

GRANDPA. Ain't that Columbus for ya? Deafest town in the Union! (*Slapping his thigh.*) They only jest heard the Confederates fired on Fort Sumter!

JAMIE. I think it's a different war, Grandpa.

GRANDPA. Hell, boy, they're all the same: men fall down and they don't get up—and nobody wins. (GRANDPA *exits up the stairs to his Attic.*)

GET-READY MAN. The Horsemen of the Apocalypse are mounting their steeds. The seal of the Book is broken and the Lion is rampant! (MARY AGNES *comes angrily toward the* GET-READY MAN, *shaking a finger at him, following him as he serpentines around the thrust.*)

MARY AGNES. How *dare* Mr. Wilson do that? We voted for him because he "kept us out of the war"!

GET-READY MAN. Don't blame me, lady. I'm just a messenger of doom. (*The sound-level of celebration is increasing from various perspectives. There are some old-fashioned auto horns beeping "AH-OO-GA," church bells are ringing.* AUNT FANNY, *of ample bosom and wearing the star spangled banner draped across it, appears in the oval picture frame. She is holding aloft a small American flag as well, patriotism personified.*)

HERMAN. Am I old enough to be drafted?

Roy. (*Worried, to* Jamie.) How far away is South America?

Jamie. You want to catch the chestnut blight? (*In the Attic,* Grandpa *is putting on his saber and Civil War fatigue-cap.* General Littlefield *strides on. He is a tall, imperious man, military to the teeth, but with a slight paunch. He is pulling on his tunic, buttoning it as he walks.* Georgiana *follows him with his military cap.*)

General Littlefield. (*Coming to the lip of the thrust.*) Ohhhh, it's a great day for America. We have declared our glorious destiny and we are going to make the world safe for democracy!

Mary Agnes. (*To* Georgiana.) Don't listen to that irresponsible madman.

Georgiana. That "irresponsible madman" is my father. (*She hands the officer's cap to the* General *who pulls it on, points a finger directly front.*)

General Littlefield. Uncle Sam wants *you!*

Charley. Maybe I ought to volunteer.

Mary Agnes. You do and I'll go cook for the Kaiser.

General Littlefield. This is the war to end wars!!!

Mary Agnes. That's crazy. Do I tell a maid: "Get the kitchen filthy—that'll clean it up"? War doesn't make peace, and dirt doesn't make clean!

Georgiana. President Wilson said it—and he's a great man.

Jamie. I thought you were a Republican.

Georgiana. My father says now we're all on the same side. (Grandpa *has strapped on his saber, clapped on his cap and has started down the stairs.*)

General Littlefield. Where are they? Where are my brave men of the Ohio State University Cadet Corps! (*Two bedraggled R.O.T.C.* Cadets *parade down the aisle, one blowing a trumpet, the other pounding a bass drum on which is emblazoned:*

O.S.U.
R.O.T.C.

*They wear rumpled Khaki uniforms and wrap-around
leggings: they are the most unsoldierly military men in
history. The trumpet player has wire-rimmed glasses and
sports a bad case of acne. The drummer is a tub of lard.*
R. *a recruiting sergeant has set up a table and a line of
volunteers is already forming. The* GET-READY MAN
dumps his bicycle and scurries to join up. L. *a girl-in-
Mary-Pickford-curls is selling "Liberty Bonds."* DOC
MARLOWE *goes up to her jauntily.*)

DOC MARLOWE. I'll take a "Liberty Bond." (*He takes
out a quarter, flipping it in the air and catching it on the
back of his hand.*) Dear young lady, I shall flip you for
it—double or nothing!

GRANDPA. (*As he passes the oval frame.*) Git yer ass
outa that picture frame, Fanny! We got a war to fight!
(*One after another, the* AUNTS *march out of the oval
frame, all waving flags and blowing kisses to the departing Doughboys.* MARY AGNES, *stunned by the military
enthusiasm, gets on the* GET-READY MAN'S *bicycle. Music
and cheers fill the auditorium.*)

GENERAL LITTLEFIELD. Lafayette—here we come!!!

JAMIE. Golly! (GRANDPA *springs to the head of the
squad of soldiers, unsheathes his saber and brandishes it.*)

GRANDPA. Remember the *Maine!* (*All the* VOLUNTEERS
and ROTC CADETS *follow* GRANDPA *up the aisle.* LITTLE-
FIELD *is left, waving with the kiss-throwing* AUNTS *and
calling: "Give 'em hell, boys! Give 'em hell!" In the
mounting war hysteria,* GEORGIANA *confronts* JAMIE.)

GEORGIANA. (*Accusingly to* JAMIE.) Why aren't you
in uniform???

MARY AGNES. (*Riding the* GET-READY MAN'S *bicycle.*)
"GET READY-Y-Y-Y . . . ! GET READY FOR
THE END OF THE WURRRR-LLLL-DD-DD!!!!!"

(*The Lights Go Out Quickly.*)

END OF ACT ONE

ACT TWO

*During the intermission the debris of the Reo has been
cleared. The protruding wire from the stove has dis-
appeared. The chandelier now bristles with bare non-
frosted electric light bulbs. There is a 2-button light
switch on the upstage wall. An electrician—a young
man in white coveralls—is on a step-ladder screw-
ing in the light bulbs. The old ice-box is gone. A
1918-modern refrigerator is in its place—an electrical
contraption with the evaporator mechanism on top.
AUNT MINNIE, haughty and dignified, is frozen for
posterity in the picture frame. CHARLEY comes
downstairs, pauses to look at the electrified chandelier.*

CHARLEY. Sa-ay! That looks just dandy! How do you
turn it up? (*The electrician crosses to the wall switch,
clicks on the chandelier.*) Well, that's just fine. (CHARLEY
*crosses to the switch, punches it on and off several times,
enjoying a new plaything.*) Great. Great. Just great. I
really feel like I'm in the 20th Century! (*The electrician
turns to reveal the lettering on the back of his coveralls:
EDISON ILLUMINATING. He hands CHARLEY a bill.*)
What's that? (*He takes it. Studies it.*) Oh. (*His joy clicks
off like an electric switch. He sighs, reaches for his wallet.
Slowly he counts out bills.*) Five . . . ten . . . fifteen
. . . (MARY AGNES *comes in the screen-door from the
back. Awkwardly she carries in 3 large paper bags full of
groceries. She sees the new refrigerator, circles it suspiciously.*) . . . seventeen . . . eighteen . . .

MARY AGNES. Charley—?

CHARLEY. Nineteen! Yes, Mary Agnes?

MARY AGNES. (*Scowling at the new refrigerator.*) I

56

don't trust it. (*The electrician nods his thanks and goes out the front door with his stepladder and tool case.*) I don't know if I'll be able to sleep at night . . . with this thing crouching in my kitchen. Listen, Charley, it growls.

CHARLEY. (*Coming into the Kitchen.*) That means it's getting cold. That's the way it works. (*He opens the refrigerator door to show her the ice-tray. Warily,* MARY AGNES *peers inside.*)

MARY AGNES. It's silly. It can't possibly keep itself cold with only this little tray of ice. The butter'll melt all over the houe.

CHARLEY. It doesn't *use* ice, Mary Agnes. It *makes* ice!

MARY AGNES. (*Thinks.*) That's unscientific.

CHARLEY. Why? It's all part of progress.

MARY AGNES. Oh, I don't mind progress. I just wish it were more—*restful.* (ROY *and* HERMAN *come up the front stoop.* HERMAN *has a baseball bat and glove,* ROY *carries a load of newspapers under his arm.*)

HERMAN. Who won today?

ROY. In baseball or the war?

HERMAN. We lost in baseball.

ROY. The paper never says exactly about the war.

HERMAN. They oughta divide the war into innings, so you'd know the score. (*In the Kitchen,* MARY AGNES *is emptying the contents of several packages into three different bowls, which she has taken out of the cupboard.* CHARLEY *watches fascinated, as she fills various dishes.* ROY *and* HERMAN *come into the Living Room.*)

ROY. (*Seeing the bulbs in the chandelier.*) Say, they got it rigged up!

MARY AGNES. (*As she stoops to place the filled bowls on the Kitchen floor.*) Is that you, boys?

ROY. No, Ma, it's General Pershing. (CHARLEY *weaves through the bowls on the floor as if walking through the points of a slalomrace.*)

CHARLEY. You're giving a dinner-party? On the *floor?*

MARY AGNES. (*Nods.*) For the mice. Mice have to eat.

CHARLEY. Fig Newtons? Walnuts? Shredded *cocoanut?*

MARY AGNES. Well, they must get awfully tired of cheese. And they're very friendly mice—so why shouldn't we be friendly right back? Besides, if I set all these bowls out here, the mice'll be satisfied—and they won't come into the Living Room.

CHARLEY. I was stupid to ask. (CHARLEY *heads into the Living Room,* MARY AGNES *follows. During the rest of the play, the family zig-zags through the bowls unconsciously, but every newcomer to the Kitchen has his own private and startled reaction.*) Boys, you're just in time for the show. Mary Agnes, sit down. (*She does, but without relaxation.* CHARLEY *goes to the light switch.*) Now. Watch! (*Dramatically.*) Let there be light! Presto! Change-o! Dingo-bat!!! (*With a flourish, he punches the switch. The boys and* MARY AGNES *watch the chandelier expectantly. The lights blaze on—but one bulb blows out with a startling flash. NOTE: Use photoflash bulb on separate circuit.*)

MARY AGNES. (*Jumping.*) Oh!

CHARLEY. Now, don't get excited. The bulb just wore out.

MARY AGNES. Already? They don't have a very long life, do they?

CHARLEY. Now if that ever happens, all you have to do is— (*He climbs up on a chair and unscrews the faulty bulb.*)

MARY AGNES. Quick—turn off the switch!

ROY. Why? (MARY AGNES *points toward the empty socket.*)

MARY AGNES. The electricity's dripping all over the house. (*She runs and turns off the switch.*)

CHARLEY. It doesn't work like that, Mary Agnes.

HERMAN. Electricity doesn't drip.

MARY AGNES. There was a bulb in there, wasn't there? And the electricity lit it up, didn't it? And if there's *no* bulb in there now, the electricity has to go *some* place, doesn't it? (*For a moment* CHARLEY *is stumped.*)

CHARLEY. Mary Agnes, you're being logical again. And you never make any sense when you're logical. (MR. BRISCOE, *the postman, plods to the front stoop, a heavy leather sack on his shoulder. He leaves several letters, bills and the* Literary Digest. *He is very very old.*)

MARY AGNES. Why not put a new bulb in?

CHARLEY. Edison Illuminating didn't leave us any. For the price I paid 'em, they should've left us enough bulbs to last all the way to 1920!

MARY AGNES. I just want you to know, Charley Thurber, that until you've got the hole plugged up— (*Pointing emphatically to the chandelier.*) —nobody pushes that button. I won't have your electricity leaking all over my family.

CHARLEY. (*Ruefully digs in his pocket for another dollar.*) Boys, run down to the store and ask Mr. Edison for one like this that lights. (*He hands* ROY *the worn-out bulb and the dollar. The boys start out the front door.* ROY *sees the mail.*)

ROY. Hey, the mail's here! (*He shuffles through it hastily, then goes pale.*) Oh, jeez—! (ROY *comes slowly back into the Living Room.*)

HERMAN. (*Trailing him.*) What's the matter?

ROY. This one's for me.

MARY AGNES. That's nice.

ROY. From the Draft Board . . . !

CHARLEY. Oh? (*With a false heartiness.*) Maybe they need you to win the war!

MARY AGNES. Shut up, Charley. (ROY *rips the envelope open, reads it hastily, then throws the paper in the air and dances jubilantly around the Living Room, kissing* AUNT MINNIE *in the oval frame.*)

HERMAN. Didja get in? (MARY AGNES *picks up the paper from the floor.*)

MARY AGNES. (*Reading.*) ". . . rejected for military service because of congenital physical defect!" (*She throws her arms around* ROY.) Roy, I'm so proud of you!

CHARLEY. (*Worried.*) What's the matter with him?

(*Now* MARY AGNES *flings her arms around her husband and kisses him.*)

MARY AGNES. *You* did it, Charley! It's the nicest thing a father could give his son! Thank you, thank you, Charley!

CHARLEY. For what?

MARY AGNES. Passing along your big flat feet!!!

ROY. (*Reflectively.*) Y'know, I'm kinda disappointed. Now that it's safe for me to be disappointed.

MARY AGNES. (*With a relieved sigh.*) Thank heaven my boy will never have to wear a uniform. (*The lights fade on the house. A spot hits* JAMIE D. L.—*in uniform. It is the malfitting regalia of the Ohio State University Cadet Corps in early 1918. If there was ever a man who was not born to the khaki, it is James Grover Thurber. In the darkness, an authoritative voice, attempting to control itself, pierces the stage.*)

WELCH. (*From off, moving on.*) Mr. Thurber! (*The light hits an area* D. R. *as* PROFESSOR WELCH *wheels on a mahogany cart containing a single old brass student microscope and a drawing pad and pencil. He wears pince-nez glasses.* JAMIE *crosses to him. The professor has a tendency to ulcers; he conceals his troubled stomach with a vest and a totally unconvincing calm. He carries a glass microscope slide and is trying valiantly to control himself.*) Mr. Thurber, I myself have prepared this slide with distilled water. There can be no question about the clarity of the specimen.

JAMIE. Yes, sir. (*The professor starts to put the slide into the microscope—notices* JAMIE'S *uniform.*)

WELCH. What kind of get-up is that you've got on?

JAMIE. It's a uniform, sir.

WELCH. Really? What army?

JAMIE. The Student Cadet Corps. Sometimes they call it the R.O.T.C. (*He squints toward an unseen clock.*) I'll be late for formation, Professor Welsh, if I have to stay too long after class—!

WELCH. (*Attempting patience.*) I am not only keeping you after class, Thurber, I am keeping *myself!* If it were not for you, I could be at home right now, smoking my pipe. But somehow I feel you are capable of passing the most elementary course in the department, Botany 401.

JAMIE. Yes, sir.

WELCH. All you have to do is see plant cells through that microscope.

JAMIE. Yes, sir.

WELCH. And draw what you see.

JAMIE. Yes, sir. But when anybody's late for drill, General Littlefield gets mad—

WELCH. (*Firmly.*) You will see cells, Thurber!—then you can go out and defend our country against all enemies, foreign or domestic.

JAMIE. Yes, sir. I'll try. (*He looks through the microscope.*) I can't see anything.

WELCH. (*Pleading.*) Thurber. All of the students in Botany 401 can see through a microscope. They are experiencing the adventure and the joy of seeing the involved and fascinating structure of flar cells. You can, too! Try, Thurber. Try!

JAMIE. I'm trying, sir. (JAMIE *tries desperately to squint through the microscope as he fiddles ineffectively with the knobs.*) But I can't see anything.

WELCH. (*Shouting.*) You can too! (*Forcing himself into a calm whisper.*) You can too. You're just pretending you can't. That is a perfectly reasonable lily-stem dissection and, as God is my witness, you're going to see it and draw it!

JAMIE. Why? It takes away from the beauty of flowers anyway.

WELCH. Beauty! My God, this is Botany! We are not concerned with beauty in this course. Only with the *mechanics* of flars.

JAMIE. Well, I can't see anything.

WELCH. (*Closing his eyes.*) Try it just once again.

Please, Thurber? (JAMIE *sighs, puts his head to the microscope again.*)

JAMIE. What am I *supposed* to see?

WELCH. A vivid, restless clockwork of sharply defined plant cells.

JAMIE. (*Suddenly.*) I do see something.

WELCH. (*Triumphant.*) Good lad! Describe it to me.

JAMIE. Well, it looks like a lot of milk.

WELCH. No!!! Your microscope isn't adjusted properly. (*He pushes* JAMIE *aside, peers fiercely through the microscope, adjusting the knobs delicately. He stands.*) There. It is now in *perfect* focus. (*He waves* JAMIE *back.* JAMIE *looks through the instrument. Reaches for the knob.*) Don't touch it—just look! What do you see?

JAMIE. (*Pause.*) Milk. (WELCH *clamps his jaw tight, and seems to be counting to ten.*)

WELCH. Do you have any difficulty in any of your other classes?

JAMIE. There's one that's even worse.

WELCH. What could that be?

JAMIE. Gym. Gymnasium.

WELCH. Migod—do they have to *teach* that?

JAMIE. It's just that they won't let you do the exercises with your glasses on, and so I keep bumping into professors and horizontal bars and swinging iron rings and agriculture students.

WELCH. Am *I* asking you to do anything unreasonable, Thurber? (*Pleading.*) Simply look into that microscope and see cells! (JAMIE *tries.*) Well? Well, Thurber?

JAMIE. I'm still trying. But—

WELCH. (*Blowing his top.*) You will see cells or I'll give up teaching. In 22 years of Botany— (*He is beginning to quiver.* JAMIE *stares at him.*) What are you staring at me like that for, Thurber?

JAMIE. You look like Lionel Barrymore getting mad, quivering all over.

WELCH. By God, if you can see Lionel Barrymore, you

can see cells through a microscope! (*Forcing* JAMIE *back into the chair.*) Now, look! And see! And draw!

JAMIE. (*Fiddling with the knobs.*) I do see something. I do. Honest I do.

WELCH. Draw! Quick!

JAMIE. (*Fumbling with the pad and sketching.*) It's a lot of flecks and specks and dots.

WELCH. Good, good, you're getting it . . . (*His eyebrows are high with. hope.*)

JAMIE. It's round, sort-of. And blinks. And seems to be looking at me. (WELCH *yanks the pad out of* JAMIE's *hand.*)

WELCH. (*With the hint of a squeal in his voice.*) What's that?

JAMIE. That's what I saw.

WELCH. (*Losing his temper completely.*) You didn't, you didn't, you didn't! That's your eye! You've drawn the reflection of your own eye! (*The lights fade on the thrust area, as* WELCH, *almost apoplectic, rolls the cart off.* JAMIE *stands alone, helpless, then he seems to remember* R.O.T.C. *and races off. Inside the Thurber house, there is a knock on the Kitchen screen-door.* MARY AGNES *opens the screen-door. A doughty middle-aged woman enters.*)

GERTIE. Mrs. Thurl?

MARY AGNES. Our name is Thurber.

GERTIE. I knew it begun with "T.H." I'm here to fill the vacancy. (GERTIE *is carrying a small carpet-bag.*) My name is Gertie Straub.

MARY AGNES. Now, Mrs. Straub—

GERTIE. Miss Straub. But nobody calls me that. I'm plain Gertie.

MARY AGNES. All right, Gertie. I want you to know that we've been having a little trouble with help lately. I guess it's because they didn't understand that when we hired help what we wanted was *help*. Not live-in aristocracy.

GERTIE. You just tell me what you want me to do and I'll do it.

MARY AGNES. Do you have references?

GERTIE. Fourteen!—from my fourteen previous mistresses—but my suitcase got lost. But I come from a good family: my brother's in the silver service. And I haven't been sick a day in my life—except when I had the intentional flu.

MARY AGNES. Gertie—I work on hunches—and I'm going to take a chance on you. (GERTIE *taps the new refrigerator.*)

GERTIE. Oh, you have one of those new doom-shaped refrigerators!

MARY AGNES. (*Significantly.*) Yes. (*Staring out the back screen-door.*) I hope you're not prejudiced against ironing, Gertie. There are about two weeks of un-ironed shirts in that basket on the back porch.

GERTIE. Oh, I love to iron. It's my specialty.

MARY AGNES. (*Quickly.*) You're hired! The pay is very good, considering we're not rich people. Room and board and two dollars a day.

GERTIE. That's very generous of you. I'll take the job. Starting right now.

MARY AGNES. Good. (*Pointing to the carpet bag.*) Is that all of your things, Gertie?

GERTIE. (*Clutching it protectively.*) This is all I'll need. (*Taking off her hat.*) Don't you worry your head about a thing, dearie. I'll start on those shirts this very minute. You just leave everything to me, Mrs. Thurl. (MARY AGNES *sighs with delight and goes into the parlor.* CHARLEY, *putting on his jacket, is coming down the front stairs.* GERTIE *stares, fascinated, at the bowls on the Kitchen floor.*)

MARY AGNES. Charley, we've got a new maid.

CHARLEY. Again?

MARY AGNES. Her name is Gertie.

CHARLEY. I've stopped remembering their names; the way they come and go, it doesn't have any practical use.

MARY AGNES. This one's different. (*Lowering her voice.*) I think she's an absolute *find*.

CHARLEY. Good. Did she have references?

MARY AGNES. Fourteen! Of course, I didn't see them. She seems to have lost them. But fourteen different places, Charley—that means she's had a lot of experience and . . .

CHARLEY. It could also mean she was fired fourteen times.

MARY AGNES. (*Suddenly worried.*) I never thought of that. (*Brightening.*) No. My woman's intuition tells me that at last we've found the perfect help. I feel so good about it I'm going upstairs and take a nice nap.

CHARLEY. (*Kissing her cheek.*) You do that, dear. And when you wake up, there's going to be a lovely surprise for you. (*He goes out the front door.* MARY AGNES *starts up the steps, humming happily.*)

MARY AGNES. She's a gem. I just know it. I feel it in my bones. (*Calling toward the Kitchen.*) Gertie, make yourself right at home!

GERTIE. (*Calling back from the Kitchen.*) Oh, I will, Mrs. Thurl. I will! (MARY AGNES *disappears into her room at the head of the stairs. In the Kitchen,* GERTIE *starts unpacking her carpet-bag: bottle after bottle of rye. She finds various places in the Kitchen to hide all the bottles, except one, which she uncorks. She clicks it against the "doom" of the new refrigerator in a toast and takes a long, happy swig. The thrust area lights up to late afternoon sunshine as* JAMIE *races breathlessly back on from* R., *awkwardly carrying a very old Springfield rifle. He looks more bedraggled than ever. He stops running as he sees* GEORGIANA *coming on from* L.)

GEORGIANA. (*Disdainfully.*) You missed drill again.

JAMIE. I thought maybe they wouldn't notice.

GEORGIANA. They always notice you at drill.

JAMIE. I'm not sure your Father likes me.

GEORGIANA. My Father doesn't like people or dislike people. He's in the Army.

JAMIE. Yeah.

GEORGIANA. In fact, all he ever said about you was— (*She breaks off.*)

JAMIE. What did he say?

GEORGIANA. He just said . . . well . . . that you're the main trouble with this university!

JAMIE. Me? (*Discouraged, he starts off.* GEORGIANA *follows.*)

GEORGIANA. Oh, I don't think he meant you, personally, Jamie Thurber. Just your *type.*

JAMIE. Thanks.

GEORGIANA. You're just not very military, that's all. I mean, even in a uniform, you don't look like a soldier.

JAMIE. (*Turning.*) What do I look like?

GEORGIANA. Well . . . (*She studies him appraisingly.*) . . . sorta like a street-car Conductor.

JAMIE. (*Blowing his cool.*) Good! Why do you have to be a TYPE? A number, nothing in a regiment! That's dumb.

GEORGIANA. Why, Jamie Thurber . . .

JAMIE. Lookit this old rifle. What's it good for? Grandpa's right: they're still fighting the Civil War! Oh, this might be okay for the Battle of Shiloh, but what's it got to do with the war in Europe? R.O.T.C.! I think there's German money behind it!

GEORGIANA. If anybody heard you say that out loud, they'd throw you in jail as a German spy.

JAMIE. (*Defiantly.*) I just said it out loud.

GEORGIANA. Well, I'm shocked. Nobody talks like that back in New Jersey. I got the idea you were sorta—well, gentle.

JAMIE. Gentle?

GEORGIANA. You know—mild.

JAMIE. Now, that's a helluva thing to say to a guy. One thing let's get straight, Georgiana—I'm not mild and I'm not gentle. Let the meek inherit the earth—they have it coming to them.

GEORGIANA. I don't understand you at all. Do you want to keep on flunking Military Science?

JAMIE. Why not? I think it's kind of a compliment. I hate rifles. I hate war. And I hate anything that even smacks of a rehearsal for it.

GEORGIANA. You be careful—or they'll kick you right out of school.

JAMIE. That might not be a bad idea either. I don't think we were meant to go together—this University and me. (*Correcting himself.*) I. Oh, someday maybe the place'll be worth something. Maybe. After they get over being interested exclusively in football and horse manure. (GEORGIANA *gasps.*) And you know what the State Legislature is trying to do? Yank Percy Bysshe Shelley out of the English books because of his un-William Howard Taft love life!

GEORGIANA. Mr. Thurber, I think you are a freak!

JAMIE. Georgiana . . . !

GEORGIANA. And that goes for your whole family, too— *freaks!!! (She turns and goes off.* JAMIE *stares after her.* JAMIE *plods off, dragging his rifle on the ground. A sepia glow hits the oval picture frame.* AUNT MINNIE—*haughty and dignified, looks straight front as if posing for posterity. Suddenly, inexplicably, she puts two fingers in her mouth, like a man, and whistles stridently.*)

AUNT MINNIE. I, Minnie Fisher Funk, was born on South High Street, I was married on South High Street, and I am destined to die on South High Street. (*She seems to become a dignified photograph again.* GERTIE *lugs a dried wash into the Living Room and sets up the ironing board. She is heating an old-fashioned iron on the stove. But she sees an interesting magazine and plops down on the sofa to read it. Simultaneously* JAMIE *re-enters from* L., *sans gun but with spirits dragging. The nettled* GRANDPA *storms on from* R.)

GRANDPA. (*Muttering.*) Goddam stupid blockheads! (*He sees* JAMIE.) Hullo, Jamie!

JAMIE. Hullo, Grandpa.

GRANDPA. If that's the way they're gonna run this country, we ain't got no more chance than a fiddler's bitch.

JAMIE. Where've ya been, Grandpa?

GRANDPA. Where d'ya *think* I've been??? The Draft Board, of course. Tryin' to enlist.

JAMIE. Oh? Whad they say?

GRANDPA. I took off my coat and said I'd whip 'em black and blue! That'd show 'em if I was too old!!! (*Squinting at* JAMIE's *ill-fitting uniform.*) What's that you got on?

JAMIE. A uniform.

GRANDPA. *Our* side?

JAMIE. I guess so.

GRANDPA. We're gonna lose! (*He starts into the house, turns on the stoop, harangues* JAMIE.) What's the idee sendin' all them soldiers to France? Makes no sense! They let me lead a division, I'd go straight to Germany. Finish the whole thing off in two weeks! (GERTIE *glances up from her magazine curiously as* GRANDPA *stomps up the stairs to the attic.* JAMIE *enters the Living Room.* GERTIE *sees him, without rising, she salutes.* JAMIE *returns the salute.*)

JAMIE. You're the new maid.

GERTIE. (*Still lounging comfortably.*) How did you know, dearie?

JAMIE. You always are. (*He passes her and goes up the back stairs to his room, where he peels off the distasteful uniform and gets into civvies. From Off* R. *comes the strident tenor beep of an electric runabout.* CHARLEY *zooms on-stage, driving it. NOTE: The electric runabout can be a golf cart with a black canopy, and dressed with black side-panels. It steers with a handle, not a wheel.* CHARLEY *is having as much fun as a kid on a Dodge-em Ride. He parks in front of the house and calls, beeping between each name.*)

CHARLEY. Mary   Agnes!   Roy!   Jamie!   Herman!

Grandpa! Look what we've got! (MARY AGNES *hurries down the front stairs.*)

MARY AGNES. What's wrong now, Charley . . . ? (*She rushes out the front stoop, sees the new electric car.*) Omigod! What is it?

CHARLEY. The latest new electric runabout—for the most modern electrified family in town! Climb aboard, I'll take you for a spin! (*Warily,* MARY AGNES *gets into the thing.*)

MARY AGNES. It doesn't even have a steering wheel—!

CHARLEY. It doesn't need a steering wheel! (CHARLEY *drives it slowly forward.* MARY AGNES *is both frightened and fascinated.*)

MARY AGNES. Isn't it dangerous, Charley?

CHARLEY. Hell, no—not unless you get it over 15 miles an hour. Backs up, too! Ever see a horse that could do that? (*They back up.*)

AUNT MINNIE. (*From the frame, shouting.*) Just keep it off South High Street! (ROY *and* HERMAN *come on;* ROY *has a new light bulb.*)

HERMAN. What *is* it???

ROY. Wow! A new Singer Electric! (GRANDPA *is coming down the stairs.*)

MARY AGNES. What makes it go?

CHARLEY. Batteries. Electricity! Smelly old gasoline, that's a thing of the past! (GRANDPA *emerges on the front stoop.*)

GRANDPA. (*Thundering to the boys.*) What the Sam Hill is that man doin' to yer mother??? (CHARLEY *brings the runabout smartly to a stop at the stoop, then helps* MARY AGNES *out with exaggerated gallantry.* JAMIE *half-dressed, has meandered down the backstairs to watch.*)

MARY AGNES. Is it ours, Charley?

CHARLEY. It's ours. It's *yours.* And this is one you'll never have to push. You *do* have to remember to get the batteries charged every two hours.

MARY AGNES. (*Disturbed.*) Every two hours? We have

to get up in the middle of the night and feed it like a baby . . . ?

CHARLEY. Only when it's running, Mary Agnes. (ROY *and* HERMAN *are crawling in and out of it.*) Now, cut that out, boys—you'll wear out the upholstery! (JAMIE *comes out, circles the new arrival appraisingly—but he is still dejected.*)

JAMIE. It's spiffy.

MARY AGNES. I guess we oughta celebrate, having this new thing in the family. But it hardly seems decent, with our poor old Reo hardly cold in its grave. (*She pats the runabout tentatively on the hood, as if she's stroking the nose of an animal.*) Nice car. Nice runabout. I'm glad you don't drink gasoline. (*She starts in the house, looks back.*) Just take care of your batteries. (GRANDPA *is measuring the machine as a horseman might size up a high-spirited colt.*)

GRANDPA. (*Looking straight into the head-lamps.*) When you've got a new wild one like this, ya gotta look it straight in the eye and let it know who's the master.

JAMIE. Grandpa, you don't have to treat it like a—

GRANDPA. (*Warning.*) Stay clear of her, boy!!! She's got a mean look!

CHARLEY. Mary Agnes'll take you for a ride in it, Pa— soon as she learns how to handle it. (GRANDPA *looks disdainfully at* CHARLEY.)

GRANDPA. Charley, I'm ashamed of ya. Where's yer *ch*ivalry??? Ya gonna leave Mary Agnes to get this thing saddle-broke . . . ? (*With a sudden spry leap—like Lee getting astride "Traveler"—he gets into the car.*) This is a job for an experienced horseman. (*All are appalled to see that* GRANDPA *is about to take off in the electric. The family moves toward him to pull him out of the machine —but he suddenly hits the foot pedal and the car lunges into motion. The others fall back to avoid being hit.*)

MARY AGNES. (*Alarmed.*) Pa!

GRANDPA. Whoa! Whoa!

JAMIE. (*Worried.*) Be careful, Grandpa!!! (GRANDPA

waggles the steering bar back and forth, the car careens madly.)

GRANDPA. Ya got the bit too tight! (*He pulls on the handle of the electric as if it were the reins of a horse. The car spurts and lunges.*)

MARY AGNES. Pa! For God's sake, it's not a horse!

GRANDPA. Ooooeeeee! This is a nasty one! Got a mind of 'er own! Keep a firm rein, or she'll throw ya— (GRANDPA *bounces about in the spastic electric.*)

ROY. Grandpa, you'll kill yourself!

JAMIE. You'll kill the *car!!!*

MARY AGNES. (*Covering her eyes.*) Oh, I couldn't stand it! Not this and the Reo, too!

HERMAN. (*Delighting in the excitement.*) Boy, you sure don't have to push *this* one—! (MARY AGNES *is hysterical.* JAMIE *comforts her.* CHARLEY *is chasing the car as if it were a runaway.*)

JAMIE. Don't worry, Mama, the batteries'll run out in two hours. (GRANDPA *curses the car as if it were an animal, slapping the seat as he would a saddle, and pulling savagely on the guide-bar.*)

GRANDPA. Flatten your ears on me, will ya??? I'll break yer spirit!— Whoa, whoa, gol-ding it, you ornery bastard! Whoa . . . Whoa! You break a leg, we'll have to shoot ya!

MARY AGNES. Stop it, Pa! You don't know what you're doing—! Stop—please!!!

CHARLEY. He doesn't know how to stop! You don't know how to drive, you old fool!

GRANDPA. Drive???!!! I druv a four-horse McCormack reaper when I was five years old, and I don't intend to be thrown by this piece of horse-flesh! (*The car dives almost directly at the front stoop, and they all scramble for cover. From the picture frame,* AUNT MINNIE *puts two fingers in her mouth and makes a piercing whistle.*)

AUNT MINNIE. (*Shouting from the oval frame.*) Don't let him loose on South High Street!

MARY AGNES. Somebody get a pail of cold water to throw at him—!

ROY. No! It's electricity—you'll short-circuit Grandpa!

MARY AGNES. (*Calls into the house.*) Dora! No, Juan-Emma! Lily! My God, what's the name of our maid today—? (GERTIE, *with a fine sense of emergency, rushes out the front door carrying the ironing board.*)

GERTIE. Don't you worry about names, Mrs. Thurl! I knew it was me you wanted! (*On* GRANDPA'S *next circuit of the thrust with the car,* GERTIE *swings at him with the ironing board.* GRANDPA *slumps forward on the guide-bar and the car coasts to a stop. The boys rush to hold it as if it were an untamed creature.* AUNT MINNIE *covers her face and disappears from the frame.*)

MARY AGNES. (*Accusingly to* GERTIE.) You've killed my father!!!!

GERTIE. (*Calmly.*) Oh, I don't think so, Mrs. Thurl. This aint' no "blunt instrument." Bein' padded like this, it probably only stunned him. See, there's no blood. (ROY *and* HERMAN *slide* GRANDPA *out of the car and put him on* GERTIE'S *ironing board as if it were a stretcher. One of* GRANDPA'S *arms falls limply. But he opens one eye as he passes* MARY AGNES.)

GRANDPA. I broke her in for ya, girl. (MARY AGNES *shakes her head, rattled but relieved.* ROY *and* HERMAN *carry* GRANDPA *into the house on the ironing-board stretcher.* ROY *has handed the new light bulb to* JAMIE. GERTIE *plods back into her room, probably for a nap.* CHARLEY *gets into the electric.*)

MARY AGNES. Put Grandpa in our room, boys. I wouldn't want to put him away in the attic in that condition.

HERMAN. You and Dad gonna sleep with Grandpa?

MARY AGNES. Of course not. We'll sleep in the attic.

GRANDPA. (*As he's carried inside.*) Saddle up that nag and ride it, girl. Don't be afraid. Show your Fisher! Show your Fisher! (*They maneuver* GRANDPA *up the stairs on the ironing board.*) I ain't no shirt! Lemme off this goddam thing. (GRANDPA *gets off the board, staggers up to the Attic.*)

MARY AGNES. (*Relieved.*) He's all right.

CHARLEY. You like the new car, dear?

MARY AGNES. Better as a car than a horse! I'm getting used to progress, Charley. I don't mind electrification as much as I thought I would. I don't trust it yet, but I don't mind it.

CHARLEY. Good, good.

MARY AGNES. But there's one thing you've got to promise me—on your sacred honor as a gentleman and a husband.

CHARLEY. What is it?

MARY AGNES. Promise first.

CHARLEY. Okay, Mary Agnes, I promise.

MARY AGNES. Let's never, never, as long as we live, have an electric toilet!

CHARLEY. What could possibly be electric about a toilet?

MARY AGNES. I don't know, but they'll think of *some*-thing! (CHARLEY *drives off in the electric.* JAMIE, *depressed, has gone into the house with the electric light bulb, stares at it, then sinks, despondent, to the couch. AUNT CHARLOTTE, a Bible in hand, her black bonnet making her look like an old-time Evangelist, has taken a pose in the oval frame, her Bible raised like the torch of the Statue of Liberty.* MARY AGNES *comes into the house, sees the forlorn* JAMIE.) Jamie? (*The lighting through the following sinks very gradually into twilight.*)

JAMIE. Yup?

MARY AGNES. What's the matter?

JAMIE. Nuthin'. (*His Mother watches him carefully. The boy turns suddenly.*) I'm a freak!

MARY AGNES. You are not!

JAMIE. She says I am.

MARY AGNES. Who says?

JAMIE. Georgiana.

MARY AGNES. (*Defensively.*) What does she know about freaks? She's not even from Ohio! Is she?

JAMIE. Naw. Some cockeyed place in New Jersey. She thinks our whole family's freaky.

MARY AGNES. Oh, I don't think we are . . . (*Glancing upstairs.*) Of course, your Grandpa's a little out of the ordinary. (*She moves toward the dejected* JAMIE.) But who wants to be ordinary? Wouldn't you hate being a Bodwell? Maybe your girl is right, we are a little bit different—

JAMIE. She's not *my* girl, Mama.

MARY AGNES. And if anybody in this family is peculiar, *I'm* peculiar.

JAMIE. You're not peculiar, Mama!

MARY AGNES. (*Strongly.*) I certainly am! I'm the most peculiar person I know! (AUNT CHARLOTTE *comes to life in the oval frame.*)

AUNT CHARLOTTE. (*From the picture.*) You're a very peculiar little girl, Mary Agnes. (*A rotogravure glow suffuses the frame, a rim-light making* AUNT CHARLOTTE'S *high-piled hair seem like a halo. Her face is pinched and pure, her voice is a high-pitched evangelical whine.*)

MARY AGNES. When I was a little girl, do you know what I wanted to do, Jamie? I wanted to go on the stage!

JAMIE. Why didn't you?

AUNT CHARLOTTE. (*Righteously.*) Exposing your body before the public for pay is an unladylike and godless urge!

MARY AGNES. I should have.

JAMIE. I know you've got talent, Mama. (*She pats his arm, but* AUNT CHARLOTTE *is firm.*)

AUNT CHARLOTTE. There is too much talk about talent in the world, and not enough about virtue.

MARY AGNES. But I listened to my Aunt Charlotte.

AUNT CHARLOTTE. Young actresses are in peril, not only of hell-fire, but of lewd Shakespearean actors, skilled in the arts of seduction.

MARY AGNES. And I listened.

AUNT CHARLOTTE. (*Raising a finger.*) God's wrath will

be visited, in His own time, upon all theatres—beginning, like as not, with those in Paris, France.

MARY AGNES. And I listened.

AUNT CHARLOTTE. (*As if to a little girl.*) You are a very good little listener, Mary Agnes.

MARY AGNES. You know why I listened? (*In a high-pitched evangelical whine.*) I was studying Aunt Charlotte's voice, so I could learn to imitate it!!! (JAMIE *and* MARY AGNES *laugh. Now* MARY AGNES *is a little distant.*) I think an actress has the best life of anybody. All the time dressing up and pretending to be somebody else. How can she ever be lonely? She has her*self*—and she's got all the people she makes up to keep her company. (MARY AGNES *takes the light bulb from* JAMIE. *She stares at it.*) Mr. Edison must've been some kind of nut to dream up a thing like *this*.

JAMIE. I bet Mr. Edison doesn't have a girl who calls him a freak.

MARY AGNES. Oh, I wouldn't be too sure. (*She puts the bulb on the table.*)

JAMIE. Professor Welch sure thinks I'm a freak.

MARY AGNES. Who's Professor Welch?

JAMIE. Botany. He's gonna flunk me if I don't draw pictures of what I see through the microscope.

MARY AGNES. Why don't you?

JAMIE. I don't see anything.

MARY AGNES. That's no reason. I can't see all that electricity sneaking around the house. But that doesn't mean it isn't there. And if I'm going to get flunked if I don't draw electricity, I'll draw electricity.

JAMIE. Mama, you can't draw electricity.

MARY AGNES. Just because you can't see it? Make up what you're supposed to see through the microscope!

JAMIE. That would be lying.

MARY AGNES. Lying? Was Michaelangelo a liar because he never saw Heaven, except in his head? But he drew a picture of it. And Dante sure as hell never saw Hell. They weren't liars, they were geniuses. People who create aren't making things up: they just manage to have a clear, factual, absolute memory of something that never happened. JAMIE *is only half-convinced.* MARY AGNES' *mind clicks into play-acting. She goes to the sofa, swirls a shawl about her shoulders and assumes a thick Mitteleuropa accent. She wheels on her son.*) Professor Velch??? (JAMIE *instantly enters into the game.*)

JAMIE. Ja?

MARY AGNES. You are recognizing me, jawohl? I am Madame Thurby, Nobel-Prize-winning woman scientist of the female sex! (*She reaches for a bud-vase, looks into it as if it were a microscope.*) Through the lens I am seeing *slithy toves!* (*She passes the bud-vase quickly to* JAMIE, *who looks down it, pretending to be* PROF. WELCH.)

JAMIE. Slithy toves? Where? Where?

MARY AGNES. Professor Velch, you are blind as a bandersnatch! (*Snatching back the vase.*) Got im Himmel, how dey are gyring und gimbling in der vabe!!

JAMIE. (*With sudden awe.*) Are you, by any chance the Madame Thurby who, after years of painstaking research with her husband, discovered— No, no, you cannot be—!

MARY AGNES. Yes, yes, I am!

JAMIE. Oh frabjous day!

MARY AGNES. Callooh, Callay!

JAMIE. I thought you were French.

MARY AGNES. Dot's Madame Curie— Ve are often confoozed. Radium—phooey! (*Flamboyantly, she peers through the bud-vase.*) But *I* haff seen what no humming-being has seen before mit der naked microscope. (*She passes the vase dramatically to* JAMIE.) Look! Look, Professor Velch—mit der eye-ball!!!! (*He peers sadly into the bud-vase, shaking his head. For the first time, he slips into his Mother's play-acting accent.*)

JAMIE. I zee nossing! Nossing! It iss time for me to take my sabbatical!

MARY AGNES. Do that, Professor Velch liebchen—and

while you're at it, learn a little English! (*They laugh.* JAMIE *kisses his Mother on the cheek.*)

JAMIE. You're fun, Mama. (*He climbs the stairs to his room. Twilight is deepening.* MARY AGNES *picks up the light bulb and seems to be stalking the chandelier, looking for the empty socket. Finding it, she pulls over a chair, climbs up on it, and warily inserts the bulb and screws it in. Then she retreats to the wall switch, punches it on. The entire chandelier lights up! In the frame,* AUNT CHARLOTTE *flips her Bible to the opening pages of Genesis.*)

AUNT CHARLOTTE. "And God said, let there be light— and the *was* light." Genesis 1-3. (MARY AGNES *is triumphant. She has conquered the age of electricity!*)

MARY AGNES. *A*-men! (*She ascends the stairs, regally, glancing back at the proud blaze of electric lights.* CHARLEY *comes in from the back, sees all the lights on, punches the switch off, and goes up the front stairs. The lighting slowly becomes middle-of-the-night moonlight.* CHARLEY *and* MARY AGNES, *during the following, get into nightclothes and crawl into the big attic bed.* HERMAN *and* JAMIE *are in their room—presumably asleep—*ROY *and* GRANDPA *are unseen in the other bedrooms. But the light still glows on* AUNT CHARLOTTE *in the picture frame.*)

AUNT CHARLOTTE. "Watchman, what of the night? Watchman, what of the night?" Isaiah, 21-11. (*She indicates the Bible.*) I don't even have to look at this, of course—I know it all by heart. (*The moonlight hits* JAMIE, *tossing restlessly on his bed.*) "When I lie down, I say, when shall I arise, and the night be gone? And I am full of tossing to and fro unto the dawning of the day." Job, 7-4.

JAMIE. Boy, that Job wasn't kidding. (*He punches his pillow, reverses it so he is is facing downstage, above the oval frame.*) Georgiana Littlefield, why did you ever have to leave New Jersey? Why don't you just go back to— (*Pause.*) To— To— (*He sits up in bed.*) Wassa name of that town? (*Trying desperately to remember.*) Something-something New Jersey. (*On tape, as if from his own head,* JAMIE'S VOICE *ticks of his thoughts. He pounds his head.*)

JAMIE'S VOICE. (*On tape.*) Walla-Walla.

JAMIE. No.

JAMIE'S VOICE. (*On tape.*) Vice-Versa. (JAMIE *shakes his head and says "No" to each suggestion from his own subsconscious.*) Hoity-Toity. Schumann-Heink. Terre Haute.

JAMIE. No . . . No . . . No, that's Indiana.

JAMIE'S VOICE. (*On tape.*) Terra Cotta.

JAMIE. That's close. But not very close. (*Now his own lips make the suggestions, but the taped voice says "No" to each one:*) Piggly-Wiggly . . . Gorgonzola . . . Prester John . . . Arc de Triomphe. . . . Holy Moses . . .

JAMIE'S VOICE. (*On tape. Over the above.*) No . . . No . . . No . . . No . . . NO! It's a city, for Pete's sake! With two names!

JAMIE. Battle Creek . . . Upper Sandusky . . . Corpus Christi . . .

AUNT CHARLOTTE. (*Helpfully.*) Sodom and Gomorrah.

JAMIE. That's not in New Jersey! (AUNT CHARLOTTE *claps her Bible shut and leaves the frame.*)

JAMIE'S VOICE. (*On tape.*) Jersey! Jersey! Jersey!

JAMIE. (*Writhing.*) JERSEY! JERSEY! JERSEY! (JAMIE *leaps out of bed.*) Herman!

HERMAN. Huh?

JAMIE. Name some towns in New Jersey! Quick!

HERMAN. (*Half-rising.*) Don't wake me up. I'm asleep. (HERMAN *falls back on his pillow.*)

JAMIE. (*Muttering, getting frantic.*) Hackensack . . . Passaic . . . Princeton . . . (*He goes up the steps to the attic room where* MARY AGNES *and* CHARLEY *are asleep.*) Pa! (CHARLEY *suddenly sits bolt upright.*)

CHARLEY. (*Startled.*) Who is it?

JAMIE. (*Urgently.*) Name some towns in New Jersey—!

CHARLEY. (*Groggy.*) Towns in—? Wha—? Whu—?

MARY AGNES. (*Wakening.*) Charley Thurber, you've been dreaming.

CHARLEY. I'm not dreaming. The *kid* came in—which one are you?

JAMIE. Jamie. It's got two names. Likes Newport News. Only that's in Virginia, I think.

MARY AGNES. (*Getting out of bed.*) Don't worry, Jamie. Every once in awhile your father has this dream that Lillian Russell is chasing him—

CHARLEY. (*Also getting up.*) I have never been chased by Lillian Russell! Grover Cleveland, yes—a few times, but never—

MARY AGNES. You ought to be ashamed, waking this boy up because you couldn't sleep—

CHARLEY. He woke *me* up.

JAMIE. I can't think of a town in New Jersey.

CHARLEY. Newark . . . Camden . . . Weehawken . . .

JAMIE. With two names!

CHARLEY. (*Humoring him.*) Elizabeth and Paterson!

JAMIE. Not two towns with one name; one town with two names! Two words, like helter-skelter.

CHARLEY. Helter-skelter. (*They are all talking at once.* ROY *comes out of his room into the upstairs hall.*)

MARY AGNES. (*Trying to be helpful.*) Minneapolis and St. Paul. St. Louis and East St. Louis.

JAMIE. (*Furious, frustrated.*) In New *Jersey*, Mama!

CHARLEY. (*Backing away from* JAMIE.) He's flipped. The kid's flipped!

JAMIE. It's like Hoboken. Or Hohokus. Only it's two words.

MARY AGNES. Hocus-pocus? Hunky-dory! Hotsy-Totsy. Upsy-Daisy. Mumbo-Jumbo.

JAMIE. No, Mama, NO! (*He comes down from the attic and runs into* ROY *in the hallway. His Mother and Father look at each other.* CHARLEY *is struggling into his clothes.*)

MARY AGNES. What are you getting dressed for? It's three-thirty in the morning.

CHARLEY. What're we worrying about New Jersey for? (JAMIE *confronts the sleepy* ROY.)

JAMIE. Quick! Name me a town in New Jersey with two names!

ROY. New York, New York.

JAMIE. In New *Jersey!*

ROY. Jersey City, New Jersey.

JAMIE. You're no help.

MARY AGNES. (*To* JAMIE.) If you just get some sleep, dear, it'll be all right.

JAMIE. Did you ever not be able to think of something, Mama, no matter how hard you tried? It's there, but you can't get at it—like something stuck between your teeth. (HERMAN *has been awakened by the noise, climbs out of bed and comes into the corridor.*)

HERMAN. Atlantic City.

JAMIE. No, there's one syllable in the first name, and two syllables in the second. Or maybe it's the other way around.

MARY AGNES. East Liverpool? West Liverpool? (*The voices of the family tumble on top of one another in quick succession:*)

MARY AGNES, CHARLEY, ROY and HERMAN. Asbury Park. Battle Creek. San Diego. Osh-Kosh. Boola-Boola. Hanky-panky. Beri-Beri. Wish-washy. Lovey-dovey! Hoity-Toity! Hootchy-kootchy! Yankee Doodle. Hula-Hula!

MARY AGNES. (*Very pleased with herself.*) Baden-Baden!

JAMIE. In New Jersey???

MR. BODWELL'S VOICE. (*Shouting from next door.*) Coney Island!

MRS. BODWELL'S VOICE. (*From next door.*) Shut up, Merle! That's in Connecticut!

MARY AGNES. Schizophrenic?

JAMIE. Too many syllables!

FAMILY. (*One-by-one.*) Sing-Sing! Mau-Mau! Boo-boo! Can-Can! See-saw!

JAMIE. (*A faint spark of illumination.*) I think it begins with a "P"!

MARY AGNES. Passaic! Paterson!

CHARLEY. I said that.

JAMIE. Maybe it doesn't begin with a "P" . . .

MARY AGNES. Pater-Noster—

JAMIE. A name, a name!

MARY AGNES. Jerome K. Jerome?

JAMIE. Of a *town!* Jeez, why couldn't she come from someplace simple like Chillicothe or Punxsutawney—?

HERMAN. That's in Pennsylvania.

MARY AGNES. Why didn't *who* come from there?

JAMIE. Georgiana.

CHARLEY. The kid has gone clean off his rocker—!

MARY AGNES. No, Charley—it's just middle-of-the-night glands. Can you remember when *you* used to have that trouble—? (*Business-like.*) Now, everybody get back to bed and get a good night's sleep.

JAMIE. (*Pained.*) I've got to think of it—!

MARY AGNES. You will in the morning. After you get some sleep.

JAMIE. I can't sleep.

MARY AGNES. Of course you can. Just keep naming over to yourself the towns in New Jersey, you'll drop right off.

CHARLEY. Now *I* can't get back to sleep.

MARY AGNES. (*To her husband.*) Go in the bathroom and brush your hair; that always calms you down. (CHARLEY *crosses toward the Bathroom* R. *Downstairs,* GERTIE *staggers out of her room. She is taking a final swig out of a bottle of rye. She gropes her way to the kitchen sink, turns the bottle upside down—empty! She lets it clank into the sink. Upstairs, the* FAMILY *freezes at the sound.*)

HERMAN. (*With mixed delight and horror.*) We got ghosts again!!! (*In the Bath,* CHARLEY *brushes his hair fiercely. Downstairs—*GERTIE *reaches under the Kitchen sink, pulls out a bottle of bleach—woops, that's not it.*

Then she finds another bottle of rye, uncorks it, and weaves happily toward the Living Room. GERTIE *draws on the liquor like a baby drawing on a bottle.* MARY AGNES *bravely goes to the head of the back-stairs.*)

MARY AGNES. (*Calling.*) Who's down there???

GERTIE. (*Pixilated.*) It's only me, Mrs. Thurl. Gertie!

MARY AGNES. What are you doing this time of night—??? (GERTIE *takes another long swig, loses her balance, falls over an arm of the sofa, toppling a lamp to the floor with a crash.*)

GERTIE. *Dusting—!* (CHARLEY *comes out of the bathroom.*)

MARY AGNES. (*Worried, to* CHARLEY.) I have a terrible suspicion, Charley. I think Gertie takes a nip now and then.

CHARLEY. She's a "gem" all right. (MARY AGNES *goes into the bathroom, reaches under the sink for a large box of dusting powder, chalk white, and starts patting it all over her face with a large powder-puff. Then she reaches for a thin, flowing dressing gown, very gossamer, on the back of the door, stares dead front into the mirror, then abruptly messes her hair so that it looks wild and demented.*)

ROY. You really are a twerp, Jamie—waking everybody up—just to find out the name of some sappy old town in New Jersey.

JAMIE. I'm sorry. I just couldn't think of it. I *still* can't!

HERMAN. Hey! I got it! *Newark!*

ROY. Oh, shut up, Herman.

JAMIE. I'm gonna wake up Grandpa . . .

CHARLEY. (*Warningly.*) Jamie . . .

JAMIE. Okay, I *won't* wake up Grandpa.

ROY. If I don't get to sleep at night, how can I expect to be a decent newspaperman?

JAMIE. You're not a newspaperman; you just sell newspapers.

HERMAN. My batting average goes down if I don't get my ten hours!

CHARLEY. And I hate to say this, Jamie, but when I don't get a full night's sleep, everybody at the State House says I act like a Democrat.

JAMIE. (*Lashing out.*) Okay. I'm the freak. Everybody else in this place is normal. Roy is William Randolph Hearst, Herman is Ty Cobb, Dad is Rutherford B. Hayes, Mama is Sarah Bernhardt, and Grandpa is Napoleon. At *least* Napoleon. I'm just Jamie Thurber and I'm pretty damn sick of it! You're all normal and I'm crazy!

MARY AGNES. I've never heard such wiggle-waggling in my life. Everybody back to bed. And the next time we're all pulled up out of a sound sleep, I hope it's about something more elevating than New Jersey! (*She shoos them al toward their bedrooms. Only* JAMIE *notices the make-up change.*)

JAMIE. (*Matter-of-fact.*) What role are you playing tonight, Madame Sarah?

MARY AGNES. The Madwoman of Thornfield Hall! (*She breaks into a shrill, maniacal giggle.* JAMIE *does not flinch; he expected it.* MARY AGNES *goes down the back stairs and crosses to the out-cold* GERTIE. *She shakes* GERTIE *awake.* GERTIE *gets one look at this apparition and starts backing away.* MARY AGNES *cackles, speaks like an old crone.*) Don't be afraid of me. I've escaped from the attic. But I'm as sane as any of you. They keep me prisoner up there because of my ardent and hapless love for Mr. Briscoe, the postman!

GERTIE. (*With a gasp.*) O-migod! (*She staggers out of the house, not looking behind her.*)

MARY AGNES. (*Calling after her.*) Ta-ta, Gertie!

JAMIE. (*Who has been watching, half-way down the stairs.*) That was very good, Mama. But why did you do it?

MARY AGNES. (*Normal voice.*) I didn't have the heart to fire her. (*They both go off to bed. The lights dip for a moment, during which* CHARLEY, MARY AGNES *and* HER-

MAN *clear. A streak of dawn appears across the sky.* JAMIE, *who apparently hasn't slept all night, is seated on his bed, pulling on a sweater. A new Aunt has appeared in the oval frame:* AUNT BESSIE. *She is very, very old. She looks about 197, but her spirit is in the mid-thirties.*)

AUNT BESSIE. (*Brightly, from the frame.*) A good night's sleep is the key to youth. (GRANDPA *emegres from* MARY AGNES/CHARLEY'S *Room, completely dressed and starts down the stairs.*) Once you're awake, the first thing you need is a large level tablespoon-full of castor oil. Opens you up! (GRANDPA *passes the oval frame just as she says this.*)

GRANDPA. (*Over his shoulder.*) You know what you're full of, don't you, Bessie? (GRANDPA *goes into the Kitchen, digs out the Post Toasties box, a quart of milk and his bowl.* JAMIE *comes down the back-stairs.* GRANDPA *squints at some fine print on the side of the cereal box.*) Hey, boy, what does that say? (*He hands* JAMIE *the Post-Toasties box.* JAMIE *jiggles his eyeglasses a little.*)

JAMIE. (*Reading from the side of the box.*) "Delicious with sliced peaches or fresh strawberries and cream."

GRANDPA. What the hell *isn't?* (MR. BRISCOE, *the post-man has come up the front stoop and is taking letters out of his sack, leaving them in the mail-box.* JAMIE *hears him and crosses, opening the front door.*)

JAMIE. Morning, Mr. Briscoe. (*Spots one letter, rips it open.*) Oh, boy.

MR. BRISCOE. (*Very ancient.*) Good news, son?

JAMIE. I've been drafted! (*A burst of activity hits the thrust area. Two white-coated doctors,* DR. RIDGEWAY *and* DR. QUIMBY, *come on from opposite sides. One is rolling on a medical cart containing stethoscopes and blood-pressure equipment. One carries a portable roll-down eye-chart.*)

AUNT BESSIE. Maybe it's the government of this country that needs a good hot enema! (*Shaking her head, she leaves the oval frame. The mailman has gone.* GRANDPA *puts his unfinished Post-Toasties bowl into the sink, seems to get a sudden inspiration, and goes out the back screen-door, disappearing.* JAMIE *races off* R. *In the thrust area, the two* DOCTORS *meet.*)

DR. QUIMBY. Good morning, Dr. Ridgeway.

DR. RIDGEWAY. Good morning, Dr. Quimby. How's everything in abdomens today?

DR. QUIMBY. Draft-evaders giving us a lot of trouble. Nails. Hairpins. Amazing what some men'll swallow to stay out of the Army!

DR. RIDGEWAY. Oughta put 'em against a wall and shoot 'em down. Dirty cowards. What I like is a good red-blooded he-man, ready to get out there and die for his country. (*Calling.*) Next! (JAMIE *comes on, stripped down to his B.V.D.'s. But he is still wearing his glasses. And he schlumps—the picture of anything but a red-blooded he-man.*) Take off your glasses. (JAMIE *does.*)

JAMIE. You're just a blur to me.

DR. RIDGEWAY. You're absolutely nothing to me. Leave your glasses here and jog twice around the hall. Then come back and I'll listen to your heart and lungs.

JAMIE. (*Putting down his glasses.*) Yes, sir. (*He runs, half-blind, around the thrust.*)

DR. QUIMBY. (*Calling off in the other direction.*) Next! (GRANDPA *comes on, in only long woolen underwear.* DR. QUIMBY's *eyes narrow.*) I didn't realize we were so desperate. Have you jogged?

GRANDPA. On my way, sonny! (GRANDPA *jogs around the thrust, in the opposite direction from* JAMIE, *waving at* JAMIE *jauntily as he passes him.*) Howdy, Jamie! See ya in the trenches! (JAMIE *staggers back to the table, squinting.*)

DR. RIDGEWAY. All right, boy. Let's examine your lungs. Take a deep breath and hold it. (JAMIE *faces away from the doctor, takes a deep breath.*) You're facing the wrong way. Your lungs are on *this* side.

JAMIE. (*Turning quickly.*) Oh, yes, sir. (DR. RIDGE-WAY *places a stethoscope to* JAMIE's *chest.*)

DR. RIDGEWAY. Say "ah".

JAMIE. Ahhhh.

DR. RIDGEWAY. Say "99".

JAMIE. (*Imitating Ridgeway.*) 99.

DR. RIDGEWAY. Sound as a dollar.

JAMIE. Yes, sir.

DR. RIDGEWAY. Pass on to abdomens. (JAMIE *gropes for his glasses.*) Wait a minute. Why, you couldn't get into the service with sight like that.

JAMIE. I know. (DR. RIDGEWAY *rolls down the eye-chart.*)

DR. RIDGEWAY. Try reading the third line of this chart.

JAMIE. What chart? (*He puts on his glasses. Now he sees!*) Z—W—T—R . . . F, I think.

DR. RIDGEWAY. (*Waving him away.*) No, no. Dismissed. Get your clothes on, report back here and I'll sign you off. You're unfit for military duty.

JAMIE. (*Uncertain to be glad or sad.*) Yes, sir. (*He goes off,* R. GRANDPA, *slightly winded, but full of piss-and-vinegar, ends his run and faces* DOCTOR QUIMBY.)

GRANDPA. All right, sonny. Gimme a uniform and I'll hightail it straight to Deutschland.

DR. QUIMBY. (*His eyes narrowing.*) Just how old are you?

GRANDPA. Stupid question. You Federal Men ask Abe Lincoln that kinda question? Or U.S. Grant? Time's-a-wastin', buddy—we got a war to win.

DR. QUIMBY Over-age. Dismissed.

GRANDPA. (*Furiously, as he stomps off.*) Sons o' sons o' sons o' sons o' bitches! Just for that, I won't tell ya my secret plan to win the war: we swarm ashore at Berlin —and fan out! (*He is gone.*)

DR. RIDGEWAY. Next! (*A draftee comes on. He is very nervous and he is shaking all over.*) Jog around the hall. (*The draftee nods and begins jogging, shaking as he jogs. The* DOCTORS *watch him, so pay no attention to* JAMIE, *who comes back on, fully dressed. He waits patiently by the rolling table, then absently picks up a stethoscope.*)

DR. QUIMBY. Oh, hello, Doctor. (JAMIE *is a bit startled, but looks at* DR. QUIMBY *steadily.*)

JAMIE. Hello.

DR. RIDGEWAY. Oh, Doctor, good to have you aboard. Glad they sent me some help. We're pretty overworked here in chest-and-lungs. (*The nervous draftee, totally winded, quivers to a stop right in front of* JAMIE.) Go ahead, Doctor. Noblesse oblige.

JAMIE. Yeah. (*He sticks the stethoscope into his ears and puts the end of it on the nervous draftee's chest. It shakes so much,* JAMIE *has trouble keeping it in place.*) Take a deep breath, then say: "Mi-mi-mi-mi-mi."

DRAFTEE. Mi-mi-mi-mi-mi . . .

DR. RIDGEWAY. Oh, very good, Doctor. Nice variation. Man gets pretty tired of the standard "ah" or "99". So do the below-the-navel men who keep having to say: "Cough!" (JAMIE *listens intently, lowering the stethoscope more to the stomach area of the draftee.*)

JAMIE. Doctor . . .

DR. RIDGEWAY. What's the problem? Need a consultation, Doctor?

JAMIE. This man seems to tick. (DR. RIDGEWAY *lays his ear to the* DRAFTEE'S *chest, thumps him, then listens with the stethoscope.*)

DR. RIDGEWAY. Sound as a dollar.

JAMIE. Listen lower down.

DR. RIDGEWAY. (*Haughtily.*) We are stictly chest-and-lungs. That is for the abdominal men to worry about. (*He points grandly to* DR. QUIMBY. *The nervous draftee quivers over to* DR. QUIMBY.)

DR. QUIMBY. (*Pointing to* JAMIE.) Who's he?

DR. RIDGEWAY. Good plumonary man, one of the best. (DR. QUIMBY *puts a stethoscope to the draftee's midsection, listens grimly.*)

DR. QUIMBY. You have swallowed a watch, my man.

DRAFTEE. On *purpose?*

DR. QUIMBY. That I can't say. If you did, you're a coward.

DRAFTEE. I'm no coward. You gotta be *brave* to eat watch.

DR. QUIMBY. Exactly what we need in the trenches—bravery! (*Calling.*) Draft this boy. (*The draftee stops shaking, shrugs, goes off.* JAMIE *taps* DR. RIDGEWAY *on the shoulder.*)

JAMIE. Doctor, don't I remind you of somebody?

DR. RIDGEWAY. Can't say that you do, Doctor.

JAMIE. There was a fella you examined a little while ago . . . a draftee. With glasses like these . . . Didn't he look anything like me?

DR. RIDGEWAY. Relative of yours?

JAMIE. Yes. No. Not exactly. A very close friend.

DR. RIDGEWAY. (*Squinting at* JAMIE.) Oh, yes, yes. I remember the one you mean. Chest and lungs normal. Terrible eyes. (*Jutting his face closer to* JAMIE.) But you don't look anything like him, Doctor. For one thing, he was a lot shorter.

JAMIE. (*Staring down at his shoes.*) *I'm* shorter without my shoes on.

DR. RIDGEWAY. (*Waving away the idea.*) No, no, I don't see the faintest resemblance between you two. (*Confidentially, chortling.*) But, frankly, Doctor, I don't see too well myself.

JAMIE. (*Nodding.*) I can see that. (JAMIE *walks away slowly and off* R. *The light fades on the thrust and comes up on the stoop of the house as the two doctors wheel off their equipment.* GEORGIANA *runs on from* L. *as* JAMIE *comes slowly on again, kicking the ground, his head down.*)

GEORGIANA. What happened at the Draft Board?

JAMIE. They didn't exactly take me.

GEORGIANA. (*Disappointed.*) Oh.

JAMIE. I guess you're not proud of me.

GEORGIANA. Not very.

JAMIE. (*Irked.*) Ya want me to be a football team, Georgiana? So you can cheer like crazy when I run out on the field—all eleven of me?

GEORGIANA. Just be *one* person. That's enough. Sergeant York is only one person. Eddie Rickenbacker is only one person. He's even from Columbus!

JAMIE. I'm not *glad* I didn't get into the Army. I didn't swallow a watch. I'm not ticking. I'm not a coward.

GEORGIANA. I didn't say you were a coward—

JAMIE. You said I wasn't Eddie Rickenbacker.

GEORGIANA. You're not. But Jamie, I think you have talent. A lot of talent.

JAMIE. No, I don't.

GEORGIANA. You always contradict me.

JAMIE. I didn't mean to contradict you. Okay. I've got talent. But for what?

GEORGIANA. Well—for what you want to *do* . . .

JAMIE. How do you know what I want to do?

GEORGIANA. I don't.

JAMIE. Neither do I. But if you say so, I've got talent for it.

GEORGIANA. (*Getting angry.*) Any time anybody says anything to you, you pull it inside out, like a dirty sock.

JAMIE. Please, Georgiana, stop trying to improve me.

GEORGIANA. Go ahead. *Be* the way you are. But don't expect anybody to understand you.

JAMIE. (*Bridling.*) What don't you understand?

GEORGIANA. About half.

JAMIE. (*A gleam in his eye.*) Let's make it a hundred percent! (*With sudden Thurber-Through-The-Looking-Glass madness.*) 'Twas brillig!

GEORGIANA. What?

JAMIE. —and the slithy toves did gyre and gimble in the wabe.

GEORGIANA. (*Backing away.*) I never took Latin—

JAMIE. Not only that, the borogoves were all mimsy! And the mome raths outgrabe!!!

GEORGIANA. That's an awful thing to say to a girl! (JAMIE *leaps up on the front stoop, waving his arms as he declaims.*)

JAMIE.

Beware the Jabberwock, my son!

The jaws that bite, the claws that catch! (*He pounces off the porch in front of her, then stalks her around the thrust.*)

Beware the Jubjub bird, and shun

The frumious Bandersnatch!

GEORGIANA. (*Bewildered.*) What's a Jabberwock?

JAMIE. Your father's a Jabberwock! And *you're* a Jabberwock—about half the time. And everybody in Columbus who does what everybody *else* in Columbus does—they're all Jabberwocks!

GEORGIANA. (*Shocked and insulted.*) Jamie Thurber, if I were married to you, I'd divorce you!

JAMIE. I'm too young to be married.

GEORGIANA. I'm too young to be divorced! (*She stomps off* R. JAMIE *goes up toward the front stoop, enters the Living Room, slamming the door defiantly.* MARY AGNES *comes out of the Maid's Room wielding a feather duster. She's even been dusting the Maid's Room!*)

MARY AGNES. (*Studying* JAMIE.) What's the matter with you?

JAMIE. I'm not exactly sure. I think a girl has just proposed to me.

MARY AGNES. Oh, that's nice.

JAMIE. The trouble is she proposed divorce at the same time.

MARY AGNES. (*Philosophically.*) Well, it's a modern age. Where've you been?

JAMIE. Down at the second floor of Memorial Hall.

MARY AGNES. What for?

JAMIE. I was seeing the Draft Board. They were more seeing me.

MARY AGNES. (*Sinking into the sofa.*) Omigod! That's the way they run the country! Grandpa's too old to go fight, Herman's too young, Charley and Roy have flat feet, I'm the wrong sex—so the U.S. of A. is going to stop the Kaiser with a boy who can't see a hippopotamus in front of him, and wouldn't shoot it if he could!

JAMIE. It's all right, Mama—they didn't take me.

MARY AGNES. (*Sighs.*) Oh, thank God. They've got more sense than I thought. (*She takes a recumbent position, draped over the arm of the sofa a-la-*GERTIE. *She makes some desultory flicks with the feather duster.*) Jamie, I want you to meet the new Maid. Her name is Mary Agnes. I'm retiring as your Mother and I'm going to work for you Father—live-in! It's the only way I'll ever get any rest around here . . . ! (*She laughs, gets up, then goes up the front stairs, flicking the feather-duster at the stair-rail. She goes off into their upstairs bedroom.* DOC MARLOWE *comes on with his battered medicine bag. He is no longer a heroic figure. His erectness is gone, the spirit is flowing out of him. With a great effort, he seems about to make one last pitch. He puts down the bag, starts to pull up the chart of the human body. He scarcely has the energy. He looks at the chart wryly, then lets it roll up like a tattered window shade. As if every bone in his body ached,* DOC *sits on his medicine bag.* JAMIE *comes down the front stoop, starts off, then sees* DOC. *Delighted, the boy changes his course.*)

JAMIE. Doc! Doc Marlowe! (DOC *sees him. He starts to stand, decides against it.*)

DOC MARLOWE. (*In a faint voice.*) Hey, Boy! He-e-ey, boy-gie—!

JAMIE. How are ya!

DOC MARLOWE. (*Lying.*) Fine! Fine—! (JAMIE *senses something is wrong, but isn't sure what. He drops to his haunches beside* DOC.)

JAMIE. Ya know that Black Hawk Liniment I bought from you for my Grandpa?

DOC MARLOWE. Did he like it?

JAMIE. (*Laughs.*) Did him so much good, he's trying to enlist in the Army—and he's way over seventy!

DOC MARLOWE. (*Faintly.*) See? Strong stuff. Now lissen to old Doc, *you* wait 'til you're seventy, boy-gie.

'Fore you enlist. Don't get suckered-in by their medicine-show pitch: bands playin', "Uncle Sam Wants You" and all that.

JAMIE. (*Sheepishly.*) They don't want me, Doc. They turned me down.

DOC MARLOWE. Oh . . . ?

JAMIE. So I guess I'm never gonna do anything heroic, like you have.

DOC MARLOWE. (*A short laugh.*) Heroic . . . !

JAMIE. Like that Tomahawk duel you had out West on horseback, with Chief Yellow Hand. (*With difficulty and pain;* DOC MARLOWE *slowly gets up, reaches into his case, hands* JAMIE *a bottle of liniment.*)

DOC MARLOWE. This is for you, boy-gie. My last bottle . . .

JAMIE. I haven't got any money, Doc. (*There's a faint twinkle of the eternal charlatan in* DOC's *eye. He fishes in his pocket for a quarter.*)

DOC MARLOWE. (*Handing the coin to* JAMIE.) We'll flip for it. Double or nothing! (JAMIE *hesitates, then flips the coin, holds it on the back of one hand, covering it with the other. The man and the boy look at each other.*) Tails.

JAMIE. (*Uncovering the coin.*) Heads!

DOC MARLOWE. I sorta thought it would be. (JAMIE *turns the quarter over.*)

JAMIE. (*Stunned.*) It's heads on both sides!

DOC MARLOWE. Handy thing for a man to have in his pocket. Never let the other fella call the turn, boy-gie. (*Achingly,* DOC *settles down on the suitcase again.* JAMIE *is staring at the phony coin. Then he looks up at* DOC *with a helpless accusation.*)

JAMIE. (*Disillusioned.*) I thought you were—you were— A great western—

DOC MARLOWE. Well, I'm not. Never was. You know how far I've been to the Far West in my whole life? (*A little laugh.*) Here. Right here.

JAMIE. (*As if somebody had kicked him in the stomach.*) You never fought that duel—?

DOC MARLOWE. Never been on horse-back. Never seen an Indian. (JAMIE *is outraged. He looks at the bottle in his hand.*)

JAMIE. Is your medicine as phony as you are? As much of a gyp???

DOC MARLOWE. (*Rising, with what strength he was left.*) NO! No, sir! It's *good* medicine! The *best!* (*More softly.*) The fella who sells it isn't too dependable. (*With difficulty he gathers up his gear, starts to move off.* JAMIE *realizes for the first time how desperately sick the man is.*)

JAMIE. Here—! (*He reaches after him.*) If this is your last bottle, use it for yourself.

DOC MARLOWE. (*Pauses.*) Even the best liniment in the world can't cure some things. (*He resumes shambling off.*)

JAMIE. You forgot your quarter—

DOC MARLOWE. (*Hoarsely.*) Keep it, boy-gie. It's a present. (*Reflectively.*) Never let the other fella call the turn. (*He starts to leave.*)

JAMIE. (*Worried.*) Doc . . . (DOC *waves as he goes off falteringly.* JAMIE *watches as* DOC *disappears. Then he goes slowly into the house through the back door. He sits at the kitchen table, studying both sides of the quarter sadly.* AUNT SARAH, *in Red Cross uniform, appears in the oval frame, posed nobly rolling bandages.* GRANDPA, *resplendent in a full Federal uniform, mounts the stoop as if he were taking Richmond.*)

GRANDPA. Damn Army and Navy! Don't know where the know-how is! (*Addressing* SARAH *in the frame.*) Allies are even worse! Those dumb British got some newspaper reporter called Churchill runnin' the Navy! (*He stomps angrily around the Living Room.* CHARLEY *comes on in the electric, beeps the horn excitedly.*)

CHARLEY. Mary Agnes! Where are the boys? Where's Grandpa? (MARY AGNES *hurries out of the upstairs bed-*

room. The telephone starts ringing simultaneously. CHAR-
LEY *leaps out of the electric, races into the house.*)

MARY AGNES. What's wrong, Charley?

CHARLEY. We just got word through the telegraph
ticker down at the State House. There may be big news
any minute!

MARY AGNES. Good or bad?

CHARLEY. Ya never know till you get it, do ya?

MARY AGNES. (*Picking up the phone.*) Thurber household—Maid speaking. (*Pause.*) It's the State House. It's
for you, Charley—! (CHARLEY *crosses to the phone.*)
Oh, I hope they don't think the Maid calls you Charley!

CHARLEY. (*Into phone.*) Charles Thurber speaking.
Yes? I'll hang on. (*Distant sounds of cheering and horns
honking.*)

MARY AGNES. What do you suppose it is?

GRANDPA. (*Disgruntled.*) The Heinies must've took Cin-
cinnati!!! Gotta git a regiment together! (*He slaps the
empty scabbard at his side.*) Who the hell hid my
saber . . . ? (*He hurries up the stairs, searches for his
saber all during the following.*)

CHARLEY. (*Into phone.*) I'm still here, I'm hangin' on!
(*The distant sound grows louder, more excited. A band,
far off, is playing "The Stars and Stripes Forever".*)

JAMIE. (*Coming out of his reverie.*) What's all the
ruckus?

MARY AGNES. Your Father's trying to find out—
(HERMAN *runs on, up the front stoop, into the Living
Room.*)

HERMAN. Hey, what's an Armistice???

MARY AGNES. (*Awed, scarcely believing.*) Armistice . . . ?

HERMAN. (*Excited.*) Everybody's jumping up and
down and yelling and shouting—and I don't understand
what they're saying.

CHARLEY. (*Overlapping, into phone.*) Yes? Yes? Shut
up, Herman, I can't hear what they're saying!

MARY AGNES. (*Embracing* HERMAN.) The war's over.

HERMAN. Hey, an Armistice is a great invention. I didn't know you could end wars just—click!—like that!

MARY AGNES. (*Goes to* JAMIE *and embraces him.*) Jamie, the war's over. (ROY *runs on, piles of newspapers under both arms.*)

ROY. Extra! Extra! ARMISTICE DECLARED!!!! (*He races into the house; there is a babble of excitement.*)

CHARLEY. (*On the phone.*) Yes? Yes? I can't hear ya— (*Turns to family.*) Will you please shut up? I'm trying to get some important news!

ROY. (*Brandishing newspapers.*) Look ! All three papers say the same thing, so it's gotta be true!

CHARLEY. (*Into phone.*) Thanks for calling me, Fred. (*Hangs up, turns to his family.*) Great news! *The war's over!*

MARY AGNES. Yes, dear. We know.

HERMAN. Everybody's going crazy over on High Street! They're dancing in the street, and kissing girls—!

ROY. Let's go!!! (*They all start out to pile into the electric—all except* JAMIE.)

MARY AGNES. Jamie—?

JAMIE. I'm OK, Mama, I just—

MARY AGNES. (*Sensing something is wrong, calling back to* CHARLEY.) Charley, you and the boys go on ahead—we'll meet you later! (*The electric glides off. In the frame,* AUNT SARAH *looks at the bandages. Shrugs. Who needs 'em? She goes off. The lights narrow on* JAMIE *and his* MOTHER D. S. *in the Living Room. The sound of the Armistice celebration is muted and very far away.*) You should be happy, Jamie.

JAMIE. Sure.

MARY AGNES. People are going to stop dying.

JAMIE. Not everybody. Friend of mine . . . (*Fingering* DOC MARLOWE'S *quarter.*) . . . he's sick. Real sick. (MARY AGNES *studies him. A little while ago* JAMIE *was just a kid. Now he seems like a man.*)

MARY AGNES. Who—?

JAMIE. (*Looking at the quarter.*) Doc Marlowe. (*Lashing out.*) He's a liar and a cheat— (*Softening, almost in tears.*) And I bet I never see him again. (*He flips the coin.*) I bet.

MARY AGNES. I know a mother is supposed to be able to explain things like that. But I— (*She stares up at the chandelier.*) —can't even explain electricity. (*She goes to the wall-switch.*) It goes on— (*She pushes the button. The chandelier blazes. Then simply:*) And it goes off. (*She hesitates, then touches the switch again, and the chandelier goes out. She comes back to* JAMIE, *sits.*) Jamie. Nobody has everything all figured out. Sometimes it seems to me that time goes by like a flash of rain. Some of the rain is clear and pretty. And some of it bounces off of rainspouts and down into the mud. I think our family was picked to be the raindrops that do most of the bouncing . . . But in the end, maybe we seep into the ground and help a hyacinth to grow, or seep even farther down and cool off some old friends who've gone to Hell! (*She has now gone from comforting to a kind of defiance.*) Jamie, there's gotta be some point to it all. God wouldn't make all this complicated world, all these complicated people—and electricity, too!—and have it all end up just a dead battery. (*She gets up.*) I want to find out what happens afterwards. I'm not in any special hurry, but I want to find out. I may be wrong, but I think it helps if you believe that what happens now— and afterwards, too—isn't all plain useless and pointless and silly.

JAMIE. (*Smiles.*) Thank you, Mama. (*He hugs his Mother and gives her a very warm kiss.*)

MARY AGNES. My, you've grown up—! (*Covering her own emotion.*) Let me see that coin. (JAMIE *hands it to her. She turns it, studying each side.*) Why, this is marvelous. Can I borrow it once in awhile, Jamie? The next time your father and I have an argument, we can just toss this and see which one of us is right. (*In the street outside,* GEORGIANA *runs on.*)

GEORGIANA. (*Calling toward the house.*) Jamie Thurber! (*The noise of the celebration comes closer, building in volume through the following. Add some scattered churchbells. The general lighting rises sharply.* JAMIE *comes out on to the stoop.*) I came to say goodbye!

JAMIE. Goodbye? (MARY AGNES *follows him out on to the stoop.*)

GEORGIANA. They don't need my Father anymore in a sensitive strategic post like the R.O.T.C. So, we're going back to New Jersey. (JAMIE *leaps off the stoop, grabs her arm.*)

JAMIE. Where? Where? Where in New Jersey???

GEORGIANA. Why, Perth Amboy, of course—

JAMIE. (*Interrupting, exulting.*) That's it!!! Perth Amboy!!! Perth Amboy!!! (*He starts to dance in the street with her.*)

MARY AGNES. (*Partly to herself.*) Perth Amboy—naturally. Now why didn't *I* think of that??? (*The electric rolls on,* CHARLEY *driving,* HERMAN *waving a flag,* ROY *tossing newspapers to the* CROWD *which is swirling about them.* GRANDPA *has found his saber and charges down the stairs, saber aloft.*)

GRANDPA. I'll stop the Kaiser on the front lawn of the State House! (*Everybody quiets for a moment.*)

ROY. (*Waving a paper.*) The war's over, Grandpa! Look! (*Leaping out of the car,* ROY *thrusts an open newspaper into* GRANDPA'S *face.*) The ARMISTICE!!!!

GRANDPA. (*Ashen.*) Armistice??? (*His saber clatters noisily to the porch steps.*) Shit!!!! (MARY AGNES *puts her around the dispirited* GRANDPA.)

MARY AGNES. (*Comforting.*) Don't take it so hard, Grandpa . . . (*She gathers the rest of the family around her.*) The war may be over in France and Germany. There may be peace all over the world. But in the Thurber household? NEVER! (*A band strikes up "THE STARS AND STRIPES FOREVER." The entire stage bursts into an Armstice Day celebration.* CHARLEY *dances a spirited polka with* MARY AGNES, *the ancient* MR.

BRISCOE *kicks up a heel with* AUNT SARAH. ROY *and* HERMAN *lift* GRANDPA *on their shoulders as the crowd swirls around them. The policemen, whistles blowing, lead the Curtain Calls, "directing traffic":* GENERAL LITTLE-FIELD *and the* CADETS *march across for their bows. The* AUNTS *are gallantly helped out of the oval frame by the cops; the maids swarm out of the Kitchen.* ROY *and* HERMAN *race down front and back stairs simultaneously.* DOC MARLOWE *comes on from* R., *as* CHARLEY *comes on from* L. *They meet in center and acknowledge applause.* JAMIE *takes his bow hand-in-hand with* GEORGIANA. GRANDPA, *upstairs, shoots off a pistol and races down to the car, then beeps the horn for* MARY AGNES' *entrance.* MARY AGNES *descends the front staircase and gets into car with* GRANDPA *and they drive slowly off as the CURTAIN FALLS. The band keeps playing. For the Final Curtain Call, a self-portrait of* JAMES THURBER *descends from the flies. The cast regroups and joins the audience in applauding him.*)

PRODUCTION NOTES

We've reached back in time to capture a piece of Americana, but the more you can convey the sense of all-of-it-happening-for-the-first-time in each performance, the more satisfying a work will emerge on your stage.

The play is very carefully shaped and structured, with the declaration of World War I ending the first act, and the hoop-la of the Armistice ending the second act. Through this we chart the maturing of Jamie, from a muddled adolescent to manhood. And through it (in collaboration with you as actors and directors) we attempt to dig beneath the surface, to find subtleties and sub-text which give the sense of a family, which illuminate the logic of illogicality, and which point up the major theme: we must protect our anomalies.

So begin with truth, avoiding any hint of the Columbus Policemen resembling Keystone Cops.

There are many facets to each character. Grandpa is not merely a time-lost eccentric. He is constantly turning the coin of character for moments of *total* lucidity and warmth. Mary Agnes goes off on trips (perhaps there is a hint of Walter Mitty in her), but she is warm and practical despite her mad logic, which sometimes seems far truer than mere facts. Each Aunt is a fierce individualist, but each has a moment of revelation, revealing a soft interior or a very human failing.

Doc Marlowe is no mere charlatan. He is a magician with words and with his medicine case. But beneath it, he longs to believe his own bunco, and perhaps wishes that Jamie were his son. He must loom large as a hero so that his fall in Jamie's eyes has impact and meaning.

It will help the "sense of family" if your set is like a bell-jar. Strive, as much as possible, to make your audience believe the Thurbers really eat, sleep, iron, dream, hear ghosts, and love each other here. There is a particular rapport among Jamie, Mary Agnes, and Grandpa: when they are in the kitchen, this is an enclave of warmth, where talk can run free, where all three seem to be on the same special wavelength.

It is important that each character, particularly the Aunts, *take stage,* indeed DEMAND stage, at each entrance.

Perhaps this is a prop-happy play, but they are important to establish the truth of time and place. The electric car can be a golf-cart, or mail truck (most colleges or universities have them), a meter-maid wagon, or a real electric car (which many collectors still have around). A slight superstructure built around a cart can give you the effective car-of-its-day.

Doc Marlowe's medicine box should be pure magic. The inside top cover should be flaming red, so that the first pass of his ten-gallon hat over it, will flip open a piece of deviltry. The legs should drop magically. The chart should spring up—so that Doc is part Houdini/Thurston as well as Buffalo Bill. The opening and the closing of the case should be done as a fabulous trick: mind-shattering sleight-of-hand.

The chandelier can be an effective prop. Suggestion: the wire should be bright red with spiraling yellow stripes. When it is poked up (from behind) through the stove, it should wiggle in sync with the poking into the chandelier.

The broken window in the front door in the first scene of the play can be accomplished effectively with a whole wired-together frame which crashes down and can be replaced by the carpenter.

The picture oval should be lit from within, if possible, with an added out-front key light. The AUNTS should all freeze as solidly as a photograph, then make a definite gesture as each springs into life. A cover for the frame, which can slide easily and unobtrusively back and forth (during moments when the attention on-stage is elsewhere) can be helpful. It should just be a drawing of a plant.

The scenes should leap-frog from one to the next in cinematic fashion. The fewer blackouts you have, the more effective the play will be.

For your program, we suggest your cover (as well as your advertising and poster logo) be the Thurber drawing: "There was a tremendous to-do." (See title page.) This and other usable drawings can be found in *MY LIFE AND HARD TIMES*, which you have permission to reproduce for lobby displays, publicity and promotion. (But NO Thurber drawings from other books may be used.) Our suggestions for usable *MY LIFE AND HARD TIMES* drawings:

"He caught the same disease that was killing off the chestnut trees"

"Police were all over the house"

" 'Dusting,' said Gertie"

"He was beginning to quiver all over like Lionel Barrymore"

Plus the cover "There was a tremendous to-do" suggested above.

SOUND

A good audio system—especially in stereo—can augment and enlarge the visual action with sound. A good mix of church bells, crowd and music, on tape, will give the declaration of war and the Armistice celebration much more impact. The sound of the chugging Reo, the approach of the street-car and the subsequent cataclysm will be enhanced by vivid sound effects. A speaker directly under Jamie's bed, using his own voice on tape, will help the reality of the Perth Amboy scene.

CASTING NOTES

MARY AGNES THURBER:

A young and vigorous 43. She has an irrepressible urge to perform, to "play-act"—but her prankishness is really a declaration-of-independence. Individuality is her banner. She has energy, warmth, deviltry. She believes implicitly in her make-believe and in her own cockeyed logic.

JAMIE:

16 or 17 when the play begins (a senior in high school), he moves on to his Freshman year in college, an indefinite 18½. This is a bright, feeling, honest young man—but he wears a perpetual question-mark on his face. He is never a "nut", or "kook" and he is anything but wishy-washy. Intelligence must peer through. He belongs to the tribe of precious anomalies which include Thoreau, Darrow and Auntie Mame. He grows, in the course of the play, toward maturity and understanding.

HERMAN:

14 when the play begins, going to 15½ by the Armistice. The younger the better, in contrast to the other brothers. A baseball bug, he has the exuberance of innocence, the open-faced bafflement of an early-day Charlie Brown. He relishes and enjoys disasters. His bright reading of "Leprosy!", "When's the funeral?" (as if he were going to a baseball game) is the key to his character.

ROY:

The family salesman, with his paper-route, goes from 19 to 21 in the course of the play. He is more careful than the others. Being the "eldest son" makes him feel he should be dignified and mature, but he never quite pulls it off. A chicken to the core.

CHARLEY THURBER:

45, is the most feet-on-the-ground member of a some-what addled family. He is firm, but gently patient. He works at the State House but he's not a conventional political figure. He has an almost boy-ish eagerness at times—as in his enthusiasm for electrifying the house. He needs his sleep. From time to time he stares at Mary Agnes in wonder: "Can I have lived with this woman for 20 years and still not understand what goes on inside that logically illogical head of hers?"

GRANDPA:

He is 77 going on 12. He is spry, bright-eyed and bushy-tailed, with a combination of madness and lucidity, which alternate at a moment's notice. He loves life and lives it to the hilt.

DOC MARLOWE:

Every boy's folk-hero of the wild west: Buffalo Bill and Wild Bill Hickcok rolled into one. It's helpful if he's tall and rangy. All energy and health at first, he turns into a shell of a man at the end. He is a con man, but a charmer.

GEORGIANA LITTLEFIELD:

18 and ice-cream-cone beautiful. There is a touch of the snob in her, but she is not stupid, and comes to have a genuine affection for Jamie. She should be stacked like a brick Armory!

GENERAL LITTLEFIELD:

Solid, substantial, dedicated, and modern as the Battle of Shiloh.

THE GET-READY MAN:

Ichabod Crane on a bicycle. He should look like Death-warmed-over, his bones as rattly as a skeleton.

PROFESSOR WELCH:

He is a smoking-pipe with a man attached. Frustrated, he attempts with all his might to control his fury. Should be able to quiver all over like Lionel Barrymore crossed with a bowl of Jello. If he doesn't have ulcers, he soon will.

DR. RIDGEWAY:
Mature, business-like, definite.

DR. QUIMBY:
A super-patriot. Fat and bearded, if possible. Balding would also help.

DORA GEDD:
Stolid, lumpy, unimaginative. Jittery from her experience at the Insane Asylum.

MRS. WEIR:
Carries herself like a lady-in-waiting to Queen Victoria. Uppity and picky and down-her-nose. 50 if she's a day.

LILY LOOMIS:
A fragile wraith of a maid. Mousey hair and personality. Constantly tearful.

GERTIE STRAUB:
Middle-aged, with the perpetual half-smile of a dedicated wino. A super-salesman of herself, she is a combination of cock-sureness and utter calm.

AUNT ESTHER:
Righteous, lean, old-maid-ish.

AUNT BELINDA:
Dowdy, busy, positive (she has the cure for everything). Overweight in contrast to Aunt Esther.

AUNT IDA:
The doom-crier of the famly. Cassandra, 1913.

AUNT FANNY:
The family extrovert. Large, domineering, an Ohio Amazon of ample bosom. Patriotism personified.

AUNT MINNIE:

Haughty and dignified, a fierce believer in predestination. Should be able to whistle with two fingers in her mouth.

AUNT CHARLOTTE:

The religious zealot, the Bible-pounder, her hair piled atop her head like a halo. Her face is pinched and pure. Her voice is a high-pitched evangelical whine. This should be the most mature of the ladies, other than Aunt Bessie.

AUNT BESSIE:

Very, very, VERY old. She looks about 197, but her spirit is in the mid-thirties.

AUNT SARAH:

The ministering angel, the Thurber Florence Nightingale. Noble and emotional.

MR. BODWELL:

The loudest voice in your company. Use a megaphone, if necessary, for the off-stage Bodwells.

MRS. BODWELL:

A distinctive, immediately-recognizable voice, with a built-in whine.

POLICE SERGEANT:

Should be as good an actor as you can find—for he establishes the whole tone of the play. Efficient, uneducated, but not stupid.

THREE OTHER POLICEMEN:

One very young, and scared to death, the other two careful, solid, dutiful.

REPORTER:

Skeptical, disenchanted, with a hat perched on the back of his head. Thinks he's Hildy Johnson.

MAIL-MAN:

Ancient. Mr. Briscoe should have arthritis and look like the weariest man in Franklin County. If he were a horse, he'd be pulling that ice-wagon.

ELECTRICIAN:

That Columbus repairman who charges an outrageous 30¢ an hour. Bored. Pure Ohio.

DRAFTEE:

Columbus' answer to Don Knotts. The most nervous man alive.

Plus:

FEMALE BOND SALESGIRL, RECRUITING SERGEANT, CARPENTER, ROTC CADET (who plays drum), and ROTC CADET (who plays trumpet).

THURBER'S SELF PORTRAIT—for final Curtain Call

* * *

We urge you to use the entire Lewis Carroll poem, JABBERWOCK, and the added comment by James Thurber in your program. You may also use, for program and publicity, our piece entitled: JAMES THURBER, THAT BEAMISH BOY.

* * *

JAMES THURBER, THAT BEAMISH BOY
by Jerome Lawrence and Robert E. Lee

James Thurber believed in the 4th dimension, maybe the 5th, and on special days even the 6th and 7th. Something sneaks in the door when you're not looking, something flies through the air and whispers to you. In that white-hot moment between dreaming and waking, Thurber found a clarity more revealing than the wisdom of encyclopedias or college professors. So do we.

Evolution throws up mutations, society produces anomalies, the inspired dissenters like Socrates or Galileo, Clarence Darrow or Henry David Thoreau. None of them used rocks or bullets or bombers to battle closed minds. They used the vorpal sword of wit and intelligence, the far keener edge of the mind to slash at the Jabberwock-dragon of conformity. And Thurber joins their mighty company.

That's why we've written this play, a slightly off-key hymn to the pertinence and the impertinence of nonsense, a psalm of life as experienced by a teenage non-conformist. Documentary? Hardly. Thurber's great friend, E.B. White, once wrote: "James Thurber never used to claim that his memories were wholly factual . . . It is easy to believe the Thurber household was an unusually active one, but surely the most tempestuous and busy spot in the whole place was the mind of little Jamie."

Thurber looked askance at the reliability of reality long before it became stylish as "Theatre of the Absurd." He and Lewis Carroll are undoubtedly the leading absurdists of the English language. Carroll's celebrated verse begins: " 'Twas brillig and the slithy toves." But

Thurber asks: "What do you mean it *was* brillig?" It still is! That's why we've called the play: JABBER-WOCK.

The Jabberwock in Thurber's life, the monstrous dragon which needed a sword in the stomach, was hypocrisy, self-deception, the lie of repetition, the toxic rumor that life is a bore. Thurber, like the young hero of Lewis Carroll's poem, slew that dragon. But the Jabberwock is a Hydra which must be slain daily. And that Beamish Boy from Columbus reminds us how it can be done!

PROPERTY LIST

Act One:
  Gas-mantle chandelier
  Umbrella stand with canes and umbrellas
  Large dictionary on stand
  Two-piece upright telephone
  Blankets and pillows
  Milk bottle in icebox
  Drip-pan under icebox
  Glasses and cereal bowls in cupboard
  Steel-rim eyeglasses (Jamie)
  Toothbrush in bathroom
  Metal pans on steps (To clatter to floor)
  Sleeping bag (Grandpa)
  Suitcase (Charley)
  Bath towel (Jamie)
  True Westerns Magazine (Under Jamie's pillow)
  Sword and scabbard (Grandpa)
  Whistles (Policemen)
  Flashlights (Policemen)
  Guns (Policemen)
  Notepad and pencil (Reporter)
  Zither (Pre-set on top of icebox)
  Suitcase, with corset dangling from it (Dora)
  Box of Post Toasties (Old fashioned variety)
  Spoon (Grandpa)
  Bicycle—Flame red (Get-Ready Man)
  Sandwich-board (Get-Ready Man)
  Tool box and tools (Carpenter)
  Specially built medicine box (Doc Marlowe)
  Paper bag (Jamie)
  Ice cream cone (Georgiana)
  Pans and scouring pads (Mary Agnes)
  Quarter (Doc Marlowe)
  35 cents in nickels (Jamie)
  Poem on sheet of paper (Aunt Belinda)
  Laundry basket piled high with clothes, boy's shirt and long
    woolen underwear on top (Mary Agnes)
  Towel (Mary Agnes)

110

Loaf of bread
Jar of jam
Bread knife and spreading knife
Herman's baseball shirt (Pre-set in icebox)
Checkers and checkerboard (Pre-set in sideboard)
Visored cap (Grandpa) (Pre-set under couch pillows)
Electrical equipment (Coils and wires, red with spiraling
    yellow stripes)
Pre-set red and yellow wire to emerge from stove
Pocket handkerchief (Jamie)
Lace handkerchief (Aunt Ida)
Family photo-album (Pre-set in stand below dictionary)
Parts of wrecked automobile:
    Fender
    Headlamp
    1917 Ohio license plate
    Flower vase with artificial rose
    Steering wheel
    Tire and wheel
    Bolts and gadgets
Winged Victory radiator cap (Georgiana)
Coffee pot and coffee cups (Pre-set on stove and in cupboard)
Small American flag on stick (Aunt Fanny)
Trumpet (ROTC Cadet)
Bass Drum, emblazoned:
    O.S.U.
    R.O.T.C.
Portable recruiting table
Portable Liberty Bond table
Small American flags on sticks (All Aunts)

Act Two:

Electric chandelier
1918-modern electric refrigerator (With evaporator on top)
Step-ladder (Electrician)
Light bulbs
Tool case (Electrician)
Wallet and large paper money (Charley)
Bill (Electrician)
Ice trays (Pre-set in refrigerator)
Two large paper grocery bags, containing Fig Newtons,
    walnuts, shredded cocoanut, etc. (Mary Agnes)

Baseball bat and glove. (Herman)
Newspapers (Roy)
Leather sack, magazines and letters (Postman)
Cart containing student microscope
Drawing pad and pencil
Pince-nez glasses (Welch)
Microscope slide
Handkerchief (Welch)
Carpet bag (Containing bottles of rye) (Gertie)
Old Springfield rifle (Jamie)
Ironing board
Old fashioned hand-iron
Magazine
Electric runabout
Light bulb (Roy)
Bible (Aunt Charlotte)
Shawl (Pre-set on couch)
Bud-vase (Pre-set on sideboard)
Empty rye bottle (Pre-set in sink)
Dusting powder (Pre-set under bathroom sink)
Silver-topped cane (Aunt Bessie)
Medical cart containing:
  Stethoscope
  Blood-pressure equipment
  Roll-down eye chart
Clipboards (Ridgeway and Quimby)
Stethoscopes (Ridgeway and Quimby)
Feather duster (Mary Agnes)
Bandages (Aunt Sarah)
Newspapers—with ARMISTICE headlines
Thurber Self-Portrait (*See sketch*)

COSTUME PLOT

MARY AGNES
Floor-length nightgown and bathrobe at the start, and bedroom slippers solid enough to throw. Then a house dress, with several apron changes. Slightly more modern house dress for Act II, a few inches above the ankle. A gossamer dressing gown with flowing "wings" so she looks like a silky bat to Gertie (To be pre-hung in the bathroom).

JAMIE
Flesh-colored athletic supporter at start, so he seems to be sleeping in the raw. Then BVD's and peg-leg trousers. An informal open-shirt. Later an ROTC uniform that doesn's fit, and leggings that lace up (but are never quite properly laced) and an overseas type Army cap. Slightly more mature clothes for Act II (in the non-ROTC sequence).

HERMAN
Knickers, a baseball shirt, a baseball cap. Long flannel pajamas at first, and a flannel bathrobe. Change for Act II, but still knickers, a shirt, and a sweater.

ROY
Long peg trousers, a floppy sweater. Pajamas he has outgrown for the opening sequence. Slightly more mature pants and a Norfolk jacket for Act II.

CHARLEY THURBER
A belted jacket and straw hat for opening, then pajamas. Peg-leg trousers and striped shirt (with gartered sleeves) for most of Act I. A change of jacket for Act II.

GRANDPA
Long woolen underwear, a full Civil War Union Army uniform, completed with peaked-cap, saber and sash. A pair of ordinary, rumpled trousers, bright red or violet suspenders. Then a full black frock coat with string tie for the mock-funeral sequence.

DOC MARLOWE
Buffalo Bill and Wild Bill Hickok suede jacket with fringe, a wide-brimmed cowboy hat, high boots and western pants. For Act II: batter them up with mud and grime, or have an alternate set which has gone to seed.

113

GEORGIANA
Sailor-like middy-blouse and pleated skirt for Act I, then pert, feminine, teenage World War I blouse and skirt. She should look sexy and sleek as an ice cream cone.

GENERAL LITTLEFIELD
Sun-tan Army uniform, with brass buttons and a military cap loaded with braid.

THE GET-READY MAN
Rags that hang together with spit and a prayer. Possibly a pullover made out of a potato sack. Bare feet and ripped trousers.

PROFESSOR WELCH
A tweed suit, complete with vest and dangling Phi Beta Kappa key. Celluloid collar and pince-nez glasses.

DR. RIDGEWAY
Three-quarter length white medical jacket, black trousers. A stethoscope dangling from his neck.

DR. QUIMBY
The same.

DORA GEDD
Nightgown at first, then a seedy overcoat pulled hastily over it.

MRS. WEIR
A Queen Mary hat, a fox-furpiece and a pseudo-elegant gown that somehow gives the impression that she is a walking overstuffed sofa.

LILY LOOMIS
Mousy clothes, drab, a living weeping-willow.

GERTIE STRAUB
Ample and forthright middle-class hired girl clothes (or "hard girl" as it was often pronounced). Apron to add, once she settles in.

AUNT ESTHER
Typical Old-Maid costume, as if stepping out of an old photograph, with a velvet band around her throat.

AUNT BELINDA
Amply padded velour gown.

AUNT FANNY
An American flag draped across her, like the Liberty Bond posters.

AUNT MINNIE
Purple for passionate belief. A period gown as if she were posing for an immortal photograph.

AUNT CHARLOTTE
Black, church-going clothes and a black lace bonnet.

AUNT BESSIE
Grey for age, her dress should be shimmery as cobwebs.

AUNT SARAH
World War I Red Cross uniform.

POLICEMEN
Their costumes should be pre-1920 policemen uniforms, which means jackets buttoned to the shoulder and visored caps. (Be certain they don't look like helmeted Keystone Cops!) Badges, brass buttons, high-button shoes.

REPORTER
Suit of the period, felt hat tipped on the back of his head.

MAILMAN
The ancient blue-grey of the dedicated public servant, with mailsack of the period.

ELECTRICIAN
White coveralls, with EDISON ILLUMINATING lettered on the back.

DRAFTEE
BVD's and bedraggled socks.

LIBERTY BOND SALESGIRL
Sailor-suit and blouse.

RECRUITING SERGEANT
Khaki uniform and broad hat.

CARPENTER
Overalls and tool belt.

ROTC CADETS
Uniforms of the period.

THE SET

The floor plan may seem formidable.

It really isn't. The play simply takes place in the interior of a house. An *entire* house, it's true—but the more that is *suggested* instead of *depicted,* the better the evening is likely to be.

The very rough sketch simply is a guide. It is a composite of various arrangements which seemed to work well in many different productions.

The thrust area is almost indispensable in this production. It is the space where the electric car cavorts, where the street scenes take place, where the Prof. Welch and draft-board sequences are inserted from R.

The photograph of the Dallas Theater Center production may be helpful, although the co-author, Jerome Lawrence, who directed, warns that this is a posed photograph of the cast on the set, not a scene from the play. The design in Dallas was executed by David Purseley.

There should be an impression of three floors, which can be achieved through a skillful use of levels and lights. *JABBER-WOCK* cannot merely be *presented;* it must *inhabit* your theatre!